DISCRIMINATIONS OLD AND NEW

Aspects of Northern Ireland Today

First published 1992
by the Institute of Irish Studies
The Queen's University of Belfast
University Road, Belfast

ISBN 0 85389 447 7

Printed by W. & G. Baird Ltd., Antrim
Cover design by Rodney Miller Associates

Discriminations Old and New
Aspects of Northern Ireland Today

Proceedings of the Irish Association Conference

Edited by Bernard Cullen

Institute of Irish Studies
The Queen's University of Belfast

ACKNOWLEDGEMENTS

The Irish Association is extremely grateful to the Gulbenkian
Foundation for funding the conference; and to the Northern
Ireland Community Relations Council and the Northern Ireland
Voluntary Trust for financial assistance with publication of this
book.

CONTENTS

EDITOR'S PREFACE

This book is the product of a conference organized by the Irish Association (with the support of the British Irish Association), which took place on 8 June 1991, in Stranmillis College, Belfast. At the conference, representatives of community groups from all sections of Northern Ireland society, together with a number of senior civil servants and other policy-makers, came together to take stock, twenty-odd years after the height of the civil rights movement, and addressed the following questions: Have some of the old civil rights grievances been satisfactorily remedied? Do some of them linger and continue to fester? Have some of them got worse? Is a more significant form of unjust discrimination in our society not against the unemployed and the poor, irrespective of their political or religious affiliation? Is the most widespread discrimination of all not against women in general, irrespective of their religion or even of their social or economic class?

The conference was organized around four workshops, concentrating on the following themes: poverty and social disadvantage; discrimination against women; discrimination in employment and unemployment; and emergency legislation and the administration of justice. The workshop discussions were preceded by two keynote addresses, by Roisín McDonough and Tom Hadden; and the conference ended with an open plenary discussion.

This book is an edited record of the day's proceedings. Because of limitations of space, the proceedings have been cut by more than half. In editing the workshop discussions, my guiding principle has been to try to retain the immediacy of the oral delivery, sometimes at the expense of grammatical niceties. My few editorial interpolations are within square brackets.

The Irish Association was founded in 1938, by Major-General Hugh Montgomery of Blessingbourne, near Fivemiletown in County Tyrone, together with Queen's University students affiliated to the Literary and Scientific Society and the Irish Christian

Fellowship, a group of students at Trinity College Dublin, Frank McDermot of Dublin (a senator and former member of Dáil Éireann), John J. Horgan of Cork, and Lord Charlemont, a former Stormont minister for education and the Association's first President. This is by no means the first time that the Irish Association has ventured into print. The overriding object of the Association has always been the promotion of contact, understanding, and goodwill among all sections of Irish people, north and south of the border; and to this end, the publication of pamphlets was a central activity from the earliest days.

In 1959, the Association embarked on a more ambitious project: an in-depth study of the causes of the antagonisms between unionists and nationalists in Northern Ireland. An interesting light has been thrown on the Unionist Government's attitude to that investigation by the recent release of the Stormont Cabinet papers for 1960. The President of the Association, the eminent Northern industrialist Sir Graham Larmor, had written to the Governor suggesting that permission might be granted for the members of the Association (including a high proportion up from the South) to visit the Governor's residence in Hillsborough on the occasion of their annual meeting in Belfast in 1961.

When his request came before the Cabinet, Prime Minister Lord Brookeborough expressed the view that it would be a mistake to agree, 'in view of the general background of the Association and the fact that some of its objectives were suspect on political grounds'. He was supported by the Minister for Home Affairs, Mr Brian Faulkner, who informed his colleagues that the Association had commissioned an inquiry into the causes of tension in Northern Ireland, and that the report would 'probably delve into allegations of intimidation, gerrymandering, discrimination in housing and similar topics, and display strong anti-Unionist bias'. Permission was denied.

The report, by Denis P. Barritt and Charles F. Carter, was published by the Oxford University Press in 1962 under the title *The Northern Ireland Problem: A Study in Group Relations.* Whether it displayed a strong anti-Unionist bias is for readers to judge. What is incontrovertible is the fact that it was one of the first publications to analyse allegations of discrimination in Northern Ireland in a scholarly and dispassionate manner.

In their introduction to that book, the authors quoted the first two aims of the Irish Association: 'to foster through the initiative of its individual members more neighbourly relations between those Irish people who differ from each other in politics and religion'; and 'to encourage respect for the convictions of others, to correct misrepresentation, and to expose intolerance and intimidation'. The present book carries on that tradition.

The Irish Association is very grateful to all who helped to make the conference so successful on the day – not least to the British Irish Association, which supported it, and the Gulbenkian Foundation, which financed it. More precise debts are acknowledged in the final page of the main text. For assistance in deciphering the tapes and preparing the edited transcript, the editor is particularly grateful to Eleanor Cullen, Julie Cullen, Jean Murray, and Eileen Webster. For financial assistance with publication of this book, the Irish Association is extremely grateful to the Northern Ireland Community Relations Council and the Northern Ireland Voluntary Trust.

PART 1

KEYNOTE ADDRESSES

CONFERENCE CHAIRMAN'S INTRODUCTION

Bernard Cullen

Good morning. Tá céad fáilte romhaibh uilig. On behalf of the Irish Association, I'd like to welcome you all to today's conference. It's very good of you all to come, especially to give up a sunny Saturday in June.

Before we get down to work, I'd like to say a few words about the Irish Association, for the benefit of those who aren't familiar with us; and a few words about why you have been invited today and what we hope to achieve.

The Irish Association for Cultural, Economic and Social Relations (to give it its full title) was founded in 1938 by Major-General Hugh Montgomery of Blessingbourne, near Fivemiletown in County Tyrone, a liberal unionist who was concerned that the two parts of Ireland were drifting further and further apart, because of the mutual suspicion and distrust that often thrive on mutual ignorance. Also involved in its foundation were Queen's University students affiliated to the Literary and Scientific Society and the Irish Christian Fellowship, a group of students at Trinity College Dublin, Frank McDermot of Dublin (a senator and former member of Dáil Éireann), John J. Horgan of Cork, and Lord Charlemont, a former Stormont minister for education and the Association's first president.

The overriding object of the Association has always been the promotion of contact, understanding, and goodwill among all sections of Irish people, north and south of the border. Then and now, the Irish Association does not have a position on the border. We include among our members both opponents of partition and defenders of partition. And I suspect we have many members (like myself) who really don't care one way or the other. We have members on the left, and we've members on the right and a lot of members somewhere in the middle. But we all share the conviction that no political border should prevent us from talking to each other and listening to each other – and especially talking and listening to those with whom we have political and religious disagreements.

I would suggest that the Irish Association has played a significant, if modest, role through the 1970s and 1980s in helping to keep alive the flame of political dialogue, both within Northern Ireland and between Northern Ireland and the Republic, through times when that delicate flame was in grave danger of being completely extinguished. We have carried out this role through our annual conferences, but for the most part in small, fairly low-key public meetings, mostly held in Belfast and in Dublin. We have succeeded particularly in persuading politicians and other public figures from the South to come north, so that we might hear what they have to say; and in persuading politicians from the North (including some who really did take a lot of persuading!) to go south, so that their voices and their points of view might be heard there in person. So the Irish Association is really a 'talking shop', with the express aim of fostering dialogue and mutual understanding, especially on the sensitive issues that divide us most deeply. And if, at the end of today's conference, you think you might find our activities worthwhile, and perhaps even exciting, as I do, you would be very welcome to join us.

Let me also say how very pleased and honoured we were when the British Irish Association, based in London but with an executive committee drawn from both sides of the Irish Sea, chose the Irish Association to arrange, with its support, a joint conference in Belfast. And I extend a special welcome to their Chairman, Dr Anthony Kenny, and their executive committee members who are with us today.

When our two committees began to plan this conference, we shared the view that we should spread our net much more widely than the 'old faithful' participants at conferences like this: namely, politicians, academics, civil servants, journalists, and so on. We were also conscious that Northern Ireland has a thriving **community** organization sector; which has grown as strong as it has, partly at least, because the normal political process has broken down. In organizing this conference, the Irish Association wishes to offer a platform to representatives of this community development movement, and an opportunity to express and discuss the range of grievances which prompted you to organize yourselves in the first place and which still concern you.

Invitations were issued to a wide range of representatives of community groups and organizations, drawn from all sections of the community and from all parts of Northern Ireland. We have tried to ensure a balance of **voluntary** community activists and **professional** community workers. We also have a number of interested but unaffiliated individuals. The most important point is that we want to hear what **you** have to say. This is why much of the day will be devoted to workshops, in which everyone will get a chance to contribute, rather than spending a whole day in a big room listening to lectures and looking at the backs of other people's heads.

Of course, you would be quite justified in saying: 'What's the point in coming along here just to let off steam? If we want to moan, sure can't we moan at home, or in our own community centre?' Well, first of all, on this occasion, we in the Irish Association hope to provide an opportunity for **cross-community** dialogue, rather than the cross-border dialogue that has been our emphasis in the past. And that, I think, would be a worthwhile achievement in itself. But as well as that, we have in our midst a sprinkling of representatives of a number of government departments and semi-government agencies against whom some of your grievances are likely to be directed, such as the Northern Ireland Office, the Department of Health & Social Services, the Department of Education, the Fair Employment Commission, the Police Authority for Northern Ireland, the Independent Commission for Police Complaints, and the Royal Ulster Constabulary. We are very grateful to them for agreeing to attend and join the workshops, primarily **in a listening capacity**. They are free to identify themselves as they see fit.

Although they have agreed to attend primarily so as to listen, I shouldn't want them to feel completely gagged. The chairpersons of the respective workshops may also invite officials to respond to specific points and bring them into the workshop discussions, if they think it appropriate. In any case, everyone will have an opportunity to join in the general discussion in this afternoon's plenary session. In this way, we in the Irish Association hope to make a modest contribution to the development of dialogue between the governed and our governors.

What of the title of our conference, 'Discriminations old and new'? A very contentious title, we were told. Well, the Irish Association has never been inclined to run away from contentiousness.

The conference could easily have been called, 'Social injustice in Northern Ireland'; and we hope the various workshops will indeed attempt to assess the extent and depth of social injustice in Northern Ireland today. But the word 'discrimination' was chosen precisely **because** it has provocative connotations in Northern Ireland; and also to establish continuity with the late 1960s.

It's an invitation to take stock, twenty-odd years after the height of the civil rights movement. That movement, in the few months when it was a genuinely non-sectarian movement, and before it came under sectarian attack and was hijacked by militant republicans, had a list of grievances and a list of demands: one man one vote; one man one house; one man one job; abolish the Special Powers Act. Twenty-odd years later, it seems appropriate to ask the questions: Have some of those grievances been satisfactorily remedied? Do some of them linger and continue to fester? Have some of them got worse?

We all have votes now – although it could be said we don't have much to vote for. Poor housing and homelessness are still real social problems, but I no longer hear complaints about sectarian discrimination in housing. Employment and unemployment, on the other hand, do continue to be divisive social problems, with a strong sectarian element. The Special Powers Act is long gone; but in terms of civil liberties, are we really any better off? Is the notion of sectarian discrimination, at least in the old Northern Ireland sense we've come to know and love, an outmoded concept? Is a more significant form of unjust discrimination throughout our society not perhaps against the unemployed and the poor, irrespective of their political or religious affiliation, who get short-changed by the state on health services, housing, education, and so on? These are just some of the questions that I hope might be addressed in our workshops today.

I listed just now the old civil rights slogans: one man one vote, one man one job, one man one house, and so on. We wouldn't get away with that today! But in those days, we simply weren't aware – at least I wasn't aware, and nobody I knew was aware – of the argument that the most widespread discrimination of all is against women in general, just because of their gender, irrespective of their religion or even of their social or economic class. Is this a relatively new form of unjust or unfair discrimination? Or is it just that we've only in latter years become aware of it? This issue will be directly addressed in one of our workshops. This posed a dilemma, because we were only too aware that women are the victims of discrimination in all realms of society, in employment and in social disadvantage in general; but after wide consultation, we decided to follow the more recent practice and provide women with the opportunity to discuss their own particular experiences of discrimination in their own workshop – and, of course, provide the rest of us with the opportunity to listen.

I am delighted to welcome our two keynote speakers this morning, each of whom brings an unparalleled wealth of experience and expertise to their respective subject. Roisín McDonough is Project Director of the Brownlow Community Trust in Craigavon, and she will be describing, and presenting as a model, the Trust's radically new approach to tackling the problem of poverty in our midst, involving a genuine partnership between statutory agencies and community representatives. Tom Hadden, professor of law at Queen's University and well-known author and civil liberties activist, drawing on his researches as a member of the Standing Advisory Commission on Human Rights, will be concentrating on the 'old' discriminations which linger since the days of the civil rights movement – the problems surrounding emergency legislation, the administration of justice, and the striking discrepancies in rates of unemployment.

Roisín and Tom, you are both very welcome.

TACKLING POVERTY: THE IMPORTANCE OF PARTNERSHIP

Roisín McDonough

Thank you for giving me the opportunity to address your conference today. The word 'poverty', and what it means, has been the site of a lot of debate over the past decade and longer. I'm not going to attempt to synopsize that debate, but I think the theme of this conference, 'Discriminations Old and New', is of direct relevance to those who either live in poverty themselves, or are actively trying to eradicate it. My main theme today will be to argue that each of us has a responsibility and a role to play in that process, be we representing the statutory, voluntary, or community sector; and that that role can only be played with the active participation of those who bear the brunt of poverty themselves.

Poverty is a contentious and uncomfortable concept. It makes people uneasy. It was the Brazilian bishop Dom Helder Camara who said: 'When I give food to the poor, they call me a saint; when I ask why the poor have no food, they call me a communist'. This quotation encapsulates to some degree the difference between the benign 'soup-kitchen' approach, however laudable that response to a crisis situation, and the necessary examination of the underlying causes of poverty and the way it is reproduced in our society.

Theories of poverty and its causes are abundant, in much reputable academic literature spanning many disparate disciplines, such as sociology, economics, politics, and social work. They range from varying levels of sophisticated 'blame the victim'-type theories through to more elaborate and considered structural analyses of the wider social and economic forces that impel people into situations of poverty. At the risk of being identified as a communist, I shall declare my hand from the outset and say that unless we develop an understanding of the forces that cause and reproduce poverty in our society, in a structural sense, we shall at best tinker around its margins, offering piecemeal individual or familial solutions; or at worst, become part of the process and relations whereby poverty is reproduced and maintained. Put simply in the vernacular: if we are not part of the solution, then we will become (if we are not already) part of the problem.

And so to the difficult area of definition: what is poverty? How do we define it in an objective sense? The European Commission, like many others, has struggled with this difficulty, but has defined 'the poor' as 'persons whose resources are so limited as to exclude them from the minimum acceptable way of life in the member states in which they live'. The Commission has stressed the multidimensional or multifaceted nature of poverty. It has also stressed its relative nature, by its reference to the living conditions of other citizens in the same society. According to this definition, poverty is the extreme form of inequality in standards of living. It is also important to note that insufficient income is only one of the characteristics of poverty. Nonetheless, it is the common denominator of all poverty and is therefore a good indicator of the extent of poverty in any area or country.

Several recent European Commission reports have quantified the growth of those living in poverty, over the decade 1975-1985, as an increase from 38 million to 44 million people; and whilst this estimate relates to 'income poverty' only, with the poverty threshold being defined as 50% or less of the average disposable income per head in the country in question, I believe that this is a useful working definition. Conceptual or definitional difficulties aside, of more serious concern is the fact that comparative figures for the twelve member states show that poverty, using the above definition, has grown faster in the poorer member states (which include both the UK and Ireland). The reports also show that the percentage of people living in poverty has grown from 6% to approximately 12% – at least, that was the last figure available, for 1985.

Now, in spite of the cherished Tory belief that a rising tide will float all boats, and a sacrosanct assertion of the 'trickle down' theory of increasing wealth improving everyone's lot, poverty has indisputably grown over the past 20 years, as the ever-growing unemployment figures also attest. Definitions of what constitutes poverty, and calculations of how many people live in poverty, are clearly politically contentious. Like the unemployment figures, which have been recalculated at least 31 times in the past twenty years in an effort to massage them downwards, notions of poverty and the figures surrounding it are in a similar vein, with government efforts seemingly more concerned to disguise the nature and extent of the problem than to tackle it seriously. One is tempted to add facetiously that by the turn of the century there may be such a massively refined and redefined definition and calculation of poverty that it will be shown that it simply doesn't exist any more.

I want to suggest, however, that there is a new poverty in Europe and in Britain – and in Northern Ireland in particular. New in the sense that it affects much larger sections of the population than before and can no longer be regarded as a problem affecting only small minorities or localized pockets within the population. It has to be treated as a mainstream policy issue, and I am pleased that the announcement by the Secretary of State, Mr Peter Brooke, in March of this year promised a government initiative that involves targeting social need and strengthening the economy as twin public expenditure priorities in Northern Ireland for the first time. I shall return to that statement shortly.

Poverty in the 1990s is also **qualitatively** different from poverty in previous decades, in that it embraces whole new categories of people. It now includes a wider range of age, gender, race or ethnicity, class, and skill categories. And this, broadly speaking, is for two main reasons: primarily, the restructuring of industry and employment, and the restructuring of the welfare state, which used to act as a collective safety net for those too old, too ill, or too young, etc., to earn an adequate income to meet their own needs. And figures have shown that poverty will increase in the peripheral areas with the advent of the single European market at the end of 1992.

Northern Ireland in particular has witnessed the growth and concentration of poverty in many different areas, such as inner cities, peripheral housing estates, in rural areas and in small towns. It now also affects significant proportions of those who find themselves in the following categories: the elderly, single parents, young unemployed, the long-term unemployed, the disabled and long-term sick, travellers, and so on. In terms of unemployment, the Catholic community is the most adversely affected, with unemployment rates for Catholics on average $2\frac{1}{2}$ times higher than in Protestant communities. Women also find themselves at the sharp end of poverty, due to an unequal distribution of houshold income weighted in favour of men who act as claimants or heads of households on their behalf. And the plight of the travelling community is nothing short of a national disgrace. All of these groups feel excluded from mainstream society – they feel that somehow there is a party going on amongst the rest of us and they are not invited; and even if they were, they wouldn't have the wherewithal to attend.

In addition to this, I want to suggest that existing programmes to help those in poverty sometimes make the problem more acute rather than ameliorating it. They are symptomatic of the failure (albeit unintended) to deliver meaningful, adequate social and economic support systems to those in poverty. Income maintenance policies, for example, are too low to allow even minimum subsistence-level living, and can lead to further problems of debt, ill health, etc.; which in turn lead to increased pressures on public personal health and social services, amongst others. Such services are also delivered in ways that stigmatize the poor and reinforce the unemployed or poor person's loss of dignity and sense of powerlessness and exclusion, rather than assist him or her in regaining confidence and autonomy.

Too many training schemes – for example, for the long-term unemployed – fail to provide skills which are needed in the local labour market, or fail in their job placement arrangements, with the result that a high percentage of the trainees slip back into unemployment and poverty at the end of training, instead of being helped on to employment. This outcome is demoralizing for those concerned and a waste of the public resources invested in the training programme. Finally, some job-creation programmes in areas of high unemployment fail because they do not relate to the indigenous technologies or the skills and potential of those looking for work, and thus do not provide jobs for those who need them most.

Having described the nature and extent of the problem, I now want to suggest some necessary ingredients or strategies that might effectively tackle it. Experience has shown that neither central government alone nor grassroots organizations alone can cope with the scale of the problem. The energies of both need to be harnessed, together with the powers and resources of area boards, local authorities, and other local agencies with the capacity to mobilize for change. Because the causes of the new poverty are more clearly economic (though the symptoms remain social), a combination of economic and social strategies is needed.

Local community development is no longer sufficient. The victims of poverty and their representatives cannot be expected to solve the problems of poverty themselves. Government community care policies, for example, and the decentralization of resources, devolving the responsibilities for services back into poor areas, so that the poor themselves become responsible for meeting their own needs without adequate resources, has only exacerbated the problem. Similarly, local enterprise strategies which focus on creating an enterprise culture amongst the more able and skilled again only exacerbate the problem of the long-term unemployed, and serve to marginalize them further within their own local communities.

What is needed is a clear political commitment and priority by central government given to anti-poverty strategies. This implies a resource commitment also. But additional resources alone will not solve the problem. Indeed, there is often a strong sense in many communities that good money is thrown after bad. I believe that Peter Brooke's recent statement provides that potential political commitment; and what we need to do now is explore more concertedly what 'targeting social need' actually means, what kinds of structures need to be set in place, and what kinds of organizations and representatives need to be involved.

Because poverty is concentrated in specific geographical areas, I am suggesting that area-based strategies can be more effective than more diffuse efforts across regions as a whole. Changes in central government policies are necessary but themselves alone are inadequate; but clearly, such agencies have a specific impact on areas where concentrations of poverty are to be found. What I wish to emphasize is that what is required is a partnership comprised of differing levels: central government, area boards, the local councils, and, most importantly, the community itself and those who actually live in poverty. I would like to give you one example of such a partnership.

Currently, I am working with an organization called Brownlow Community Trust, which is funded under the Third European Programme to 'foster the economic and social integration of the most disadvantaged'. You will notice that the word 'poverty' doesn't appear in the official title of the programme, and that was because the British Government objected to the word 'poverty' being included in it officially. Anyhow, the project began in 1990 and will run until 1994, with an allocated budget of £2 million over this four-year period. Like most European programmes, national government had to provide matching funding. The table depicts the kind of partnership and level of representation on the board of the Trust, and I think several points are worth noting.

BROWNLOW COMMUNITY TRUST BOARD MEMBERS

Northern Ireland Voluntary Trust	2 representatives
Brownlow Community Development Association	4 representatives
Southern Health & Social Services Board	2 representatives
Southern Education and Library Board	2 representatives
Northern Ireland Housing Executive	2 representatives
Craigavon Borough Council	2 representatives
Brownlow Limited	2 representatives
Department of Health & Social Services	1 representative
Department of the Environment	1 representative
Department of Economic Development	1 representative

Plus 4 additional community representatives who shall be directly elected at an open public meeting in the area, on an annual basis. These four community representatives should not represent any particular community organization or association, though as individuals they may be involved in local groups. Rather they should represent the wider interests of the whole community.

4 co-optees to represent the interests of the target groups with whom the Trust will be working:

(a)	Long-term unemployed	1 representative
(b)	Young unemployed	1 representative
(c)	Women	1 representative
(d)	Children	1 representative

The composition of the board of management of Brownlow Community Trust can be broken down thus:

Statutory representatives	11
Community representatives (including Brownlow Limited's Community Director)	13
Neither statutory nor community (i.e., NIVT and Chief Executive of Brownlow Limited)	3
	———
Total	27

The Board is a company limited by guarantee, and each member is an equal partner and director. Community representatives form the majority; and the Board as a group takes all decisions regarding the financial control of the programme and the strategies adopted to tackle poverty. The issues of inter-agency co-operation and co-ordination of services for the benefit of the community can be (and I believe are beginning to be) addressed. The token exercise of consulting the community without giving them full and equal access to the decision-making processes that affect their local area has been avoided by accepting the community's right to have an effective say in statutory policies and agency service delivery, on an equal basis. This mixture of central government, area boards, the local authorities, the private sector, and the active participation of the community within a geographically defined area is a structure and a type of partnership which has not happened elsewhere before – at least, not to my knowledge. But lest I paint too rosy a picture of such a partnership, as a panacea which will cure all, I should add some correctives.

Such a specific model may not be the most appropriate for all areas in which poverty is concentrated. The partners may be different elsewhere; but the mixture, I believe, is a necessary prerequisite. Partnership, however, is not simply an aggregate of discrete individuals cemented together in an artificial or formal structure. It is a process of development which implies a commitment to shared goals and strategies which have to be worked out.

People in poverty, who are rarely consulted about policies, and even more rarely asked to participate actively in decisions and policies which impact on their lives, are understandably suspicious of the motives of statutory bodies; and government agencies are also afraid that community activists will demand the impossible and behave irresponsibly, in their eyes. Such perceptions are grounded in real undeniable fears, and genuine partnership can only evolve on a basis of trust. Yet the central responsibility in any such partnership rests with those who have control of resources, to listen actively to community demands; and such listening may mean putting increased resources into poor areas, as well as bending mainline programmes to make them more directly amenable to the needs of those whom they are supposed to serve.

I have already spoken of the importance of the participation by the community not being token. But communities themselves are not homogeneous entities with a united agenda of common interest. This is particularly true of Northern Ireland, where communities are divided along political and sectarian lines, with differing attitudes to the state itself. The issue and history of sectarian resource allocation within Northern Ireland needs to be urgently addressed in a more radical manner. The legacy of government policies has adversely affected working-class Catholic communities disproportionately, but they have also begun now to bite more severely in poor, deprived, working-class Protestant communities, who are facing rising unemployment rates. And within both these communities, single parents, women, and children who live in poverty are the most acutely affected of all, through either not having sufficient income when the income directly comes to them, or having their access to it mediated by others.

So, what I'm saying is that community representation in a partnership structure should not be drawn solely from those already active in the community or in voluntary organizations. The task is much more difficult than that. It must also be crucially drawn from the ranks of those in poverty who may have been (and may still be) inactive members of the community – namely, the unemployed themselves, single parents, the disabled, travellers, and so on, depending on the nature and type of poverty existing in the area. So, what kind of strategies are needed to tackle poverty in a concerted manner? I don't know. Nor does my project have all the answers; and it is important to state that a four-year anti-poverty programme is only a beginning. Strategies are long-term developments, with clear objectives and means by which to achieve them. But I would like to offer some suggestions.

The long-term unemployed are the most difficult group to reach. Any programme, if it is to be successful, must concentrate on offering support and personal development, so that confidence can be rebuilt and a sense of self-esteem achieved. Training or retraining which does not try to telescope this initial phase will be more successful; but clearly work, at the end of the day, is the most crucial need. In the short term, immediate measures to generate jobs in the service sector, through improvement in local systems of social support, are required.

The one example I wish to concentrate on is the crucial importance of offering adequate, cheap, high-quality child care, particularly for single parents and women, if we are to be seen to be serious about devising strategies for improving family incomes and lifting women and children out of poverty. Such child-care or

day-care centres are the *sine qua non* of women's access to education, training, and employment initiatives. The demand for them
has been articulated by many women in local areas over the past
twenty years and more. The fact that Northern Ireland does not
have a single statutory-provided day-care centre anywhere is an
appalling indictment; and I would urge those responsible to tackle
this immediate problem. We have the worst system of child-care
support in the whole of western Europe.

In the medium term, it may also be possible to generate jobs in
the construction industry and the building trades: for example,
through improvements in housing conditions and the environment. The Department of the Environment and the Housing
Executive should actively consider allowing local firms, employing
local people in an area, to gain employment without having to
tender for larger contracts; and where large contractors are needed,
they should stipulate that they should employ directly a set percentage of local labour in any works programme. This has been
done before, by many local authorities in England, without contra-
vening fair employment practices or other legislation. All the
above should be harnessed to longer-term measures to increase
private and public investment in areas which will help improve the
income, skills, and job opportunities of those in poverty. I have
mentioned some examples of the kinds of activities that are needed.
You may think of others; and, as I have already stated, although I
offer these strategies (to a degree) in a prescriptive sense, they are
not exhaustive.

I would like to conclude my address today by suggesting a
couple of ways in which we could move forward. The first is in
relation to the government's promise of making available additional resources to target the areas of greatest social need. I would
urge them to learn the lessons of similar programmes in the past,
and indeed the lessons from their own current initiatives into
'making Belfast (or Derry, etc.) work'. Such programmes should
not allow statutory agencies to abdicate their responsibilities because of substitute funding which is made additionally available
under such initiatives. Of course, such monies which are not tied
to any one agency can be used more imaginatively, less bureau-
cratically; but the danger is they can and have become a substitute
or a way of augmenting the hard-pressed mainline programmes of
the statutory sector itself.

The second point I wish to make is also crucial, and it is this:

unless we directly involve local communities and people who live in poverty other than in a token manner, such programmes will be seen as yet more in a successive stream of top-down initiatives which do not meet the extent of real needs felt in local communities. A sense of ownership of such programmes by people is vital. That, I would suggest, is the first step on the road to tackling the major social and economic issues that keep people who live in poverty where they are today.

And finally, I would like to leave you with the thought that in the efforts to eradicate poverty, we will also hopefully eradicate what has been called the poverty industry. People like myself, I hope, will become increasingly redundant, as local people become empowered and gain an effective say in running their own lives. Thank you.

THE OLD DISCRIMINATIONS: EMERGENCY LEGISLATION, THE ADMINISTRATION OF JUSTICE, AND EMPLOYMENT

Tom Hadden

I was brought up in Portadown, and that has stamped my personality and my gut reactions. In the places where I was brought up, there were certain unwritten and often unspoken assumptions. One of them was that Catholics had too many children, and that if they insisted on having too many children – well, that was their look-out, and it was up to us to look after ourselves and make sure that we weren't outvoted in the future. And if that involved a little bit of discrimination – well, so be it. Another was that, while you were quite nice to Catholics, you didn't really have very much to do with them. I remember the consternation that I produced at home one evening when I came back after a dance in Belfast where I'd been chatting up a girl. I didn't actually know she was a Catholic, but everybody else did, and I was severely taken to task. It wasn't the sort of thing that you did in Portadown in those days.

I hope I've moved along a little bit from there. I went over to England for a number of years, and I picked up some liberal ideas there. Since I've come back here, though, I've come to the view that liberal ideas in England are mainly for show. I've become deeply cynical about the commitment of the British State and the British Establishment to ideals of human rights and justice.

I remember being particularly annoyed when I was called to the Bar in England. It was just after the introduction of internment. One of those crusty old judges stood up. Most of the rest of us were black and were being sent out to the colonies. We were given a stirring speech about the merits of the Common Law tradition, and how we were to go out and teach the people out there the great values of British justice and the British commitment to civil rights and civil liberties. I happened to be the oldest, so I had to give a speech in reply. I remember getting more and more angry as I heard this old fogey going on. So I got up and gave him a piece of my mind about what was going on in Northern Ireland – it was in, I think, September 1971. I still sometimes get very angry at the way in which members of the British Establishment portray themselves as being committed to peace and justice and human rights. Often it's not very deep; and that's something I want to come back to.

In the '70s, I came back here and worked at Queen's. I worked with Kevin Boyle and Paddy Hillyard, doing some rather pedestrian academic work on the nature of security abuses. After about a decade of chewing over the statistics on sentencing and internment and Diplock trials, we eventually came to the conclusion that there wasn't going to be a solution by means of changes in security systems alone. So, in the 1980s, Kevin Boyle and I shifted our attention to more political matters. I was also involved in the early stages of the Committee on the Administration of Justice, trying to draw together various disparate groups who were trying to make political progress on security issues. After a few years of CAJ work – they've come along a lot since I left them! – I was appointed in 1986 to the Standing Advisory Commission on Human Rights. A lot of what I have to say is based on the work which I've been involved in there. First of all, work on discrimination; and secondly, work on the control of abuses of emergency powers.

I still don't think – Kevin Boyle and I have come jointly to this conclusion – that the answer lies in getting security policies right, or in dealing with discrimination. We have come to the conclusion that we are not going to make enough progress on those matters to resolve our problems unless we can also get some sort of political settlement. My primary commitment at the moment is to that. I would agree also with almost everything that Roisín McDonough has said. But, regrettably, I have to come back to the order of events. I think the priority has to be first to deal with our own particular localized difficulties, of unemployment, terrorism, and the political impasse; and then, perhaps, when we have resolved some of those, we can turn our attention to the equally important issues of poverty and other forms of discrimination. We need to get our priorities right: we have to deal with the old forms of discrimination which are still with us, before we can move on to the newer forms that Roisín has been talking about.

Security and Emergency Legislation
What I want to do now is to suggest some issues of emergency law

and practice that you may usefully talk about in your groups. But first of all I want to say what my general stance on the issue of security is. My stance is something like this. We have got ourselves into such a mess, with paramilitaries and murders and bombs, that it is unrealistic for us to say that we can rely simply on ordinary laws. Whether we like it or not, we are going to have some special laws to deal with the fact that people are going around shooting each other, and shooting policemen, and planting bombs, and so on. It is unrealistic to say that there is no difference here, that all we need is an ordinary system of law. But when we are introducing emergency powers, we do need to be very careful that we bring along with them safeguards to see that they are not abused. This is the line that the Standing Advisory Commission has been taking over the years. I think it is the correct line; and I make no apology for going through some of the issues from that point of view.

What I have in mind, and what SACHR has been saying for years, is that on each of the issues which cause problems, there is a possible way forward – not to solve all the problems, but to increase confidence among both communities in the work of the security forces, to reduce the level of antagonism between the security forces and local communities, and, in the longer term, if we can manage to get some sort of political settlement, not to defeat the paramilitaries, but to make it quite clear to the paramilitaries that there isn't really any point in their continuing. I am opposed to anybody who suggests that there is a way of defeating the paramilitaries by increasing the use of tough security tactics. I don't think we can resolve the problems until we have got some sort of political stability, and then we will, all of us here, be able to say to the paramilitaries: 'Look, there isn't any point in your continuing with your operations. We haven't defeated you. We aren't going to rub your noses in the dirt. But there isn't actually any point in continuing your campaign, so will you please stop'.

My list of issues is in a logical, academic order: out in the streets first of all, then moving along to the police station, and then to the courts. Let's begin with lethal force.

Lethal force
It seems to me that it is very bad strategy and policy for members of the security forces to shoot terrorists when they can be arrested. The reason is that when members of paramilitary bodies are shot

dead, their colleagues are annoyed, and their communities are annoyed if there are suspicions that perhaps the true story wasn't quite as it was put forward in the initial press statements. As a result, there is a natural commitment to avenge those deaths. When two or three members of a paramilitary body are shot dead, the likelihood is not that that will decrease the number of shootings, but that it will have the immediate effect of increasing or, at any rate, sustaining the level of killing between the security forces and the paramilitaries.

That doesn't involve me saying to you that I am always against shooting people. I am not against shooting people, if those people pose an immediate threat to my life, to your life, or to the lives of members of the security forces. But my suspicion is that the law that we have on lethal force in this country (and also, incidentally, in the Republic) is such that it is possible for the security forces to create situations in which paramilitaries may be shot dead lawfully, but in circumstances in which they could have been arrested.

My reasons for thinking this are that British and Irish law on the use of lethal force is very different from the law which prevails in international human rights instruments. We have got a rule based on 'the reasonable use of force', whereas the international standard is 'such force as is absolutely necessary in order to prevent death to other people'. I suspect that that crucial difference is used by some people in the security forces to justify operating in a way which is likely to result in people being killed when they might have been arrested.

What should we do about it? The Standing Advisory Commission has suggested three things that we need to do about it. The first is a code of conduct. SACHR has produced a code of conduct for the use of lethal force, which adopts the international standards rather than the looser 'reasonable' British/Irish standard. SACHR also thinks there should be a more sensible sanction. The difficulty at the moment is that, if the rules are breached, the only possible sanction is a charge of murder. I don't believe that a charge of murder is likely to succeed, or indeed just, in many of the circumstances in which people are shot dead in disputed circumstances. To insist on a charge of murder makes it almost impossible for the Director of Public Prosecutions to bring charges, makes it highly unlikely that anybody will ever be convicted, and results in there being no effective sanction against those soldiers and policemen who do overstep the mark.

The second thing that SACHR has suggested is, therefore, that there should be a sensible range of sanctions: that murder charges should be restricted to those cases in which there is evidence that there was a deliberate pre-arranged attempt to 'take out' some paramilitary personnel without justification; that in other circumstances there should either be a charge of manslaughter, where unreasonable force was used, or alternatively, a charge of breach of the code of practice which SACHR has suggested.

Thirdly, there is the question of inquests. I don't think anybody who has seen the way that inquests operate in this jurisdiction can be happy with the current rules. The Lord Chancellor has on occasions said that our rules are no different from those in Britain. That is arrant nonsense. The rules are substantially different from those in Britain. They are in breach of accepted international guidelines for inquiries in cases of the use of lethal force by security forces, and they need to be changed, in at least three ways.

First, there needs to be express provision for an inquest to be held quickly, if charges are not quickly brought in cases where charges are appropriate. I have suggested a month or two months. I'd be prepared to stretch to three months. But to have inquests running on two, three, four, or five years after the event seems to me to be totally unjustifiable. Secondly, we need to change the rules so that those who are responsible for the killings can be called to give an account of what they did. That is built into the international standards, which have recently been approved by the United Nations. This issue was dealt with in the *McKerr* case, in which the House of Lords delivered what I consider to be a disgraceful judgement. It is now up to Parliament to bring us back to a proper set of procedures in accordance with international human rights law.

The third change concerns verdicts. Coroner's inquests have been prevented, in this jurisdiction, by what seem to me to be challengeable means, from bringing in verdicts. The Coroners Act says that juries are to bring in verdicts. But the authorities have said: 'No, you can't bring in verdicts; you can only bring in findings, and the findings cannot give any indication about what you think about the lawfulness or otherwise of the killing'. It seems to me that that is probably the most challengeable part of the law on inquests here; though ultimately I think we need some new legislation, or at least some new Coroners Rules.

Arrest and Search

The second issue concerns powers of arrest and search. I have no
objection (given the number of people running around with guns
and bombs) to being stopped, to having my car boot opened, to
being asked who I am and where I come from. It seems to me that
that's not unreasonable in the circumstances. The worries that I
have are that some of these powers are being abused. One of the
important areas of abuse is harassment: that is, the continual
rearrest of people, not for the purposes of seeing whether they
have a gun with them, not for the purposes of properly question-
ing them as to what they've been up to, but for the purposes of
making it clear that they are on the list, and that they should desist
from associates, or from operations, or from the kind of life-style
that they are involved in.

SACHR has suggested some ways in which the powers could be
more tightly controlled to ensure that people aren't continually
rearrested. One of the safeguards would be to require a formal
record to be made every time somebody is arrested under the
various powers. Another safeguard would be to say that a person
can't be arrested continually for interrogation on the same evidence. That is the rule which prevails in the Republic. It seems to
me to be a sensible rule to allow one bite of the cherry if you have
information, but not to allow a person to be repeatedly arrested and
detained for four or five days on the basis of the same suspicion.

The third safeguard – and I think this is the most important one
– is to require video and audio tape recording of what goes on
in interview rooms. SACHR has been having a long series of
disputes and arguments with the authorities on this matter. It
seems to me perfectly obvious and acceptable that what goes on in
an interview room in Gough or in Castlereagh [holding centres]
should be recorded on video tape. The purpose is both to protect
the police from unjustified allegations that they are beating people up, and also to protect those who are being interviewed from
being beaten up.

The official argument, as I understand it, is that we couldn't do
that because a lot of interviewing is undertaken for the purposes
of obtaining information from people who are prepared to give
that information; and that any video record or audio tape record
would inevitably come out in some way. The implication is that
people who are hauled in and who are assisting the security forces
are encouraged, or at any rate permitted, to make a complaint, so

that they can come out and say to their mates: 'I was done over; I was ill-treated, and I made a complaint'. That is apparently the reason why the authorities are now saying they cannot possibly introduce this kind of safeguard.

I personally am not convinced by that argument. It seems to me that the general communal feeling that things are not always as they might be in Castlereagh and Gough is much more likely to stem the flow of information to the security forces than the faint possibility that one or two people might possibly not assist the police when they are arrested, for fear that if they made a complaint three or four or six months later, somebody else other than the authorities might get access to a video recording which might show that they had actually talked to the police. It seems to me that that's a bit far-fetched. I think we need to stand firm and say that the proper safeguard is video recording first, tape recording later, of what goes on in interrogation centres, because that will increase communal confidence in the police and will assist in the flow of information which is the best way of preventing terrorist operations.

Finally, under this heading, I'll say one thing about the seven-day arrest power. It seems to me quite unacceptable that the British Government should hold out against the European Court of Human Rights over the possibility of an extra two or three days of detention, when the only issue is whether or not there should be some judicial control over the extension of detention. It seems to me that there is absolutely no justification for the British Government to continue its derogation on that particular point, when there are several different ways in which the requirements of the European Court could be met. We could have various forms of judicial control over extensions of detention; or we could reduce the length of detention to the permitted period, four or five days. There are some people who are against judicial control in this kind of case. The judges are said not to be willing to get involved. But sometimes we have to stand up and say: 'Part of the judicial function under the European Convention of Human Rights is to do this job, and that is what we pay you to do'. We should not allow the judges to say: 'Well, we don't really want to get involved in this sort of operation'.

Trial
I don't want to say a lot about Diplock courts. I've never been absolutely committed to juries. It seems to me, in our particular

circumstances, that the likelihood of getting a fair and just verdict
in the more important cases is just as high from a judge as from a
jury, which would be open to intimidation and pressure and
perhaps even prejudice. I think it would help if we had collegiate
courts. I've always argued for two rather than three judges, in
order to meet the argument that there aren't enough judges. Two
also has the advantage that you can, without actually saying so,
have one of each. It also avoids the problem of two outvoting one.
But I don't think that juryless Diplock courts are in themselves a
major problem.

Evidence

There are, however, some aspects of Diplock trials which cause me
some concern. I think that we have gone a little bit too far in
altering the rules of evidence. I have no objection to altering the
rules to the extent that people are obliged or put under pressure
to give an explanation of why they were in a particular area in
suspicious circumstances, or why guns were found in their house.
That seems to me to be a reasonable rule. But not so the way in
which the authorities have introduced it.

First of all, they introduced the new rules under the Criminal
Evidence Order a couple of years ago, for all criminal cases, when
really their arguments were that the special rules were needed in
terrorist trials. I think they did that in order to avoid having to go
through the parliamentary process in any real sense. It's that sort
of move that makes people like me question the bona fides of
those who are introducing some of these measures. They say: 'Yes,
of course, we are committed to principles of human rights'; and
yet they seem continually to adopt measures in a way which makes
it difficult for those who wish to argue about safeguards to have
any influence on what is being done.

The safeguard that the Standing Advisory Commission has argued for in this context is that before any questions are put from
which an adverse inference can be drawn, suspects should have a
right of access to their lawyer. The lawyer can then explain to the
person what the issues are, and explain whether he or she should
wait until trial, or whether he should give an account to the police,
and so on. That seems to me to be fair.

Prisons

I don't want to say a lot about prisons. SACHR has been having discussions on the issue of transfer of prisoners. My own view is that the way to get easy transfer of prisoners is to accept in principle that the prisoner should serve the sentence he or she would have served where he or she was sentenced. In other words, if you were sentenced in Britain, you would continue to serve the sentence that you got in Britain under British rules for remission or under British rules for release from life sentences, but you could be transferred to a Northern Ireland prison and serve the sentence there. That seems to me to be the first step towards making for easier transfer. In the longer term, it would help if all the rules could be brought into line.

Paramilitaries

I want to end this part of my talk by saying something about the question: 'What are we going to do about the paramilitaries who are carrying out the most atrocious actions?' They are killing people without proper trials, even from their own ranks, laying bombs all over the place, shooting people in front of their children – the list is unending of the human rights abuses that are carried out by paramilitary bodies on both sides. Though it's not part of the international human rights agenda, it has always seemed to me that there is some merit in attempting to set some limits to the use of force by insurrectionary bodies.

There is currently a proposal for a code of conduct, which is being discussed by the International Committee of the Red Cross and others, which would attempt to set rules for both sides – both the paramilitaries and members of the security forces. This would allow paramilitary bodies like the IRA or the UVF to be called to account as to whether or not **they** have respected internationally accepted standards in the conduct of their operations. This approach is not liked by Government, because it implies that there may, in certain circumstances, be some legitimacy in the operations of insurgent bodies. But of course there **is**, in some circumstances, some legitimacy, when all other avenues have been explored, or when they are faced by dictatorships and security forces who pay no attention to any rules. Even when there is no such justification for paramilitary activity, there may be some merit in exploring whether or not, as well as having a code of conduct for members of the security forces in using lethal force, we could have some rules as to what ways of carrying out paramilitary operations are so totally unacceptable that everybody will agree that we must do something about calling into account those who continue to act in that way.

Discrimination in Employment

The second area of old discrimination is, of course, discrimination in employment. I think it is accepted that there was some discrimination under the Unionist regime, and that that resulted in differential unemployment rates. The figure that everybody quotes (which, as far as I gather from my researches on the matter, has been pretty static for the last 20–30 years) is $2^1/2$ times male unemployment among the Catholic community compared with the Protestant community. The first attempt to deal with this unemployment discrepancy legally was the Fair Employment Act in 1976. That Act didn't have a great impact; I think mainly because most of the focus initially was on individual complaints. Most people now accept that that is not the way to deal with this issue. It is so difficult to establish the facts in particular cases, and so difficult to get people to pursue complaints effectively, that you don't really achieve much by way of individual complaints, though you have to have provision for it.

It wasn't until the Fair Employment Agency got down to carrying out sectoral investigations – or investigations into particular firms – that the extent of the problem really began to emerge, and action became possible. The most important of those investigations was the Civil Service one. I mention it because I think the fact that the Fair Employment Agency carried out an inquiry into the Civil Service had an important impact on what is happening now. The Civil Service, who had always held themselves up as being above suspicion, found that everything was not perhaps quite as they had thought it to be, and they took some action. As a result, there have been very substantial changes in the patterns of Civil Service employment.

When I got involved in this sphere in 1986, the Standing Advisory Commission was already engaged on a major report on the law in relation to discrimination. I had to do a crash course on anti-discrimination law; and SACHR spent hours and hours arguing about what we called 'the tie-breaker' – whether or not it was legitimate, in circumstances in which two people of equal merit came forward, to give the job to that person who was under-represented in the work-force (a Catholic in a company where there were too few Catholics, a Protestant in a company in which there were too few Protestants). SACHR didn't really resolve the issue. It said: 'Perhaps we'll come back to this one in our five-year review'. The Government, though, wasn't particularly interested in the argument over tie-breakers, or any forms of reverse discrimination. Instead, with its experience of what the Civil Service had found to be necessary, it decided that the way forward lay in monitoring: 'Find out what the situation is in your firm, and that will be the best incentive for doing something about it'.

The Standing Advisory Commission had been relatively low-key in respect of monitoring. I was quite surprised when the Government took our suggestions on monitoring, beefed them up, made them compulsory, and gave the new Fair Employment Commission powers to require comprehensive monitoring by all the larger firms in the Province. I think that the Government's decision in that should be welcomed. They went further than many people thought they would go; and I hope that the kind of monitoring that the FEC are now undertaking will encourage more and more employers, like the Civil Service, to take serious action to deal with the situation.

I want to finish off with a few figures on differentials in employment. I started off with the long established fact that the rate of unemployment for Catholic men is $2^1/_2$ times higher than for Protestant men. This kind of measure – of $2^1/_2$ times, or 2 times, or $1^1/_2$ times – is bandied around a lot. I've said that I share the idea that monitoring the situation is a good start to doing something about it. But I'm not sure that the $2^1/_2$ times multiplier is the best way of monitoring the overall situation, because that kind of ratio is suspect in statistical terms. It varies in its impact, depending on the overall level of unemployment. I've done some rough calculations to show the nature of the problem. I've focused on males, because it is in respect of males that the big divergence occurs.

The current unemployment rate for men is around 23%, and there is a differential of $2^1/_2$ times between Catholic and Protestant men. That means that there are approximately 50,000 Catholic men unemployed, and approximately 30,000 Protestant men unemployed. But if the overall male unemployment rate was only 17%, that would mean that 15,000 fewer Catholic men would be unemployed compared with only half that number of Protestants, even if the $2^1/_2$ times differential were unchanged. That is a bigger reduction in Catholic male unemployment than would occur if the $2^1/_2$ times differential were reduced to $1^1/_2$ and the overall rate remained at 23%. The actual effect of a change in the differential depends on the overall unemployment rate.

That is why I'm worried about everybody hanging on to the $2^1/2$ times multiplier as being the only possible measure of progress. If, of course, we were able to get down to a $1^1/2$ times multiplier as well, that would be even more satisfactory. But it does seem to me that there is some merit in thinking in terms of overall numbers, rather than getting hooked on: 'How much progress have we made? Have we got down to $2^1/2$ times? To 2.45? To 2.3?', without understanding that the impact of these figures is highly dependent on the overall rate of unemployment.

The advantages of thinking in actual numbers can also be illustrated. For example, if we were to try to get to what the Standing Advisory Commission suggested should be the target, a reduction to a differential of $1^1/2$ times in five years, we would have to transfer about 12,000 Protestants from being employed to unemployed, and vice versa for Catholics. That's not a huge number in terms of overall employment. It is also, incidentally, very like the differential in employment in the security industry. The implication is that, if in some way we were able to secure equality of employment in the security forces and the security industry and in prisons, we would probably at a stroke achieve the Standing Advisory Commission target of the reduction of the Catholic rate of unemployment from $2^1/2$ times to $1^1/2$ times.

Conversely, and as a corollary, while the huge imbalance in the security forces is maintained, we are going to have to make even more progress in all the other sectors, so that there is a higher proportion of Catholics in non-security-related employment than you would expect in relation to the overall situation. That's a problem, and I offer you those figures to think about in your employment seminar, because it seems to me that we should be thinking in terms of overall strategies: how are we to create and distribute those extra 12,000 jobs that we need in order to meet that initial target of reducing the discrepancy in unemployment rates from $2^1/2$ times to $1^1/2$ times?

PART 2

WORKSHOP DISCUSSIONS

POVERTY AND SOCIAL DISADVANTAGE

Brian Garrett (The Irish Association):
No matter what we do on the subject of poverty, it seems to me that there are problems of definition and problems of deciding the best form of action. I'm delighted to see that our group has a balance, in Northern Ireland terms, and also a breadth of experience. I'd rather hoped that you would tell us a little bit about your experience, where it's relevant.

Poverty is a subject which is inclined to make us all feel beaten and despondent. Maybe we could start by taking up Roisín's point and asking whether or not poverty is just merely material. It seems to me that Roisín's lecture clearly said 'no', it's cultural and other things besides. It appears to me to be mainly about the distribution of power in society, whether it be in terms of material goods, or education, or skills, or whatever. That seems to me to be as much of a definition as we can get. And whether one has access to those levers in one's lifetime seems to me as good a definition as any of whether or not one is disadvantaged or otherwise.

I want to relate our discussion to where we are (we're in Belfast); and the second point is whether or not the issues that Roisín was addressing have a bearing upon the two communities' attitudes to each other. Whether or not, in other words, those areas which suffer most from a sense of deprivation are likely to be the areas in which violence and antagonism are bound to prevail. I ask that as a question, because I don't know if there is any obvious answer. And related to that, whether it affects voting behaviour in the longer term, because that relates to what Tom Hadden was saying about the need to look at political action as well.

So, having said all that, I wonder if I could start by inviting the representative of Work West to speak about your experience in the environment you now work in. And perhaps we could then take one of the various Shankill representatives. I've singled these out simply to get the discussion going. And then I thought we might go on to your experience, Eileen, in Derry.

Joe McVey (Manager, Work West, Belfast):
Work West, on the Glen Road, is one of six enterprise agencies in West Belfast. Enterprise agencies are places where people can come, receive advice, and set up their own business. We are meant to be a job creation agency. We try for a very high profile. We're fairly well funded compared to a lot of other groups here. We've a very good staff. But what concerns me increasingly is that although we're doing valuable work, and we have had some success in the area of job creation, the people of the area (the people living in areas such as Lenadoon and Suffolk) don't know who we are or what we do; and we have less and less relevance to the people that surround us.

With regard to funding, initially we got grants through LEDU [the Local Employment Development Unit] and through the International Fund for Ireland; but we also have to charge rents and charge for other services. I'm manager of the centre, and there's a board of management made up of the usual crew of accountant, property developer, solicitor, and business people: people who have businesses in the area or people who were brought up in the area and have developed their own successful businesses.

Constance Short (Co-operation North):
What are their politics? When you say 'west', is the board Catholic, is it Protestant, or is it everything?

Joe McVey:
The board is very strongly Catholic.

Constance Short:
And is the Church involved?

Joe McVey:
Yes. There are two church representatives on our committee. One from the Church of Ireland, who never appears; and one from the Catholic Church, who appears two or three times a year.

Joyce McCartan (Women's Information Drop-In Centre, Lower Ormeau Road, Belfast):
You said there about the community not knowing what you were

doing. That is because there's not many people in the community involved on the committee. Sometimes the people in the community say that they're not capable, but I think you have to involve the people in the community in what you're doing; let them see it's for them. That's where the failure is there, because there's not enough people in the community involved.

Brian Garrett:
Could I just ask you: what would you say your main success to date was – if there was such a single main success?

Joe McVey:
That we have developed an enterprise agency on a piece of ground that was owned for fourteen years by the Government, and nothing happened in that fourteen years until the community itself got the centre up and running; and that it has helped, so far, maybe eighty local people create businesses for themselves. And because of the work my group has done, the Government has now come in and built a factory beside us. We have proved that developments can happen in that area. It's not a no-go area.

Brian Garrett:
So you've broken the barrier of disbelief by bringing employment. Could I now ask someone from one of the Shankill or Protestant West Belfast groups to say what your experience is and what you do.

Gusty Spence (Shankill Activity Centre, Belfast):
If any good has come from the troubles, it certainly has been the rise of community groups within the Protestant areas. Before the troubles, community groups were almost unheard of. It was left to the constitutional politicians, who invariably failed. They didn't deliver. Unfortunately, people had no recourse except to take it stoically, because if they had criticized the politicians in any shape or form, as I've said often, they would have been seen to be traitorous or taigish, less than confident in the Unionist Government. The border would've fallen, the Jesuits would have moved in, and all hell would have broken loose. But now the people are beginning to do it for themselves.

The Shankill is still something of a disaster area, but we're getting there. We're talking about 63% unemployment, according to a recent survey by Touche Ross for the Greater Shankill Development Agency. Thirteen of our children, out of 373, passed their 11-plus last year. That's all. Thirteen out of 373. We have almost double the national average of old-age pensioners. That's because – and fair play to them and thank God for them – the old people said: 'We're not moving, we're going to stay here'. And they still form the backbone of the Shankill population.

The Shankill is a queer place, inasmuch as there's a certain amount of misguided pride. But some positive things have come forward. This is the paradoxical situation. The people are doing the double in the Shankill now, where twenty years ago it would've been completely unheard of. That was a thing that Catholics did! They realize now that they are underprivileged, they realize now how much they have been conned. The Catholic/nationalist population (and fair play to them) have had some successes: whatever they ask for, they get it, or they get it themselves. In some instances, they see themselves as a state within a state. And now the people of the Shankill are beginning to do it for themselves.

The exciting part is that those of us – if you don't know, I'll tell you, I served nineteen years in Long Kesh – those of us who were connected with paramilitary organizations, in some instances with the most extreme paramilitary organizations, a long time ago realized that violence was not the way forward. And we returned prisoners are working constructively – and it happens in both sections of the community, thank heaven – we're working constructively and giving a lead. Now, those people who have been there for a while might not like it – that's just bad luck about that. If they don't come with us, then we'll take them with us. But the Shankill's on the march!

Brian Garrett:
What's the success story here? Is it, as you suggest, that the Shankill community now realizes they've got to do it for themselves?

Gusty Spence:
The success story – with all due respect to the church gentleman – is that the Protestant churches didn't really concern themselves with the secular aspect of the people. But now we have gingered them up, to some degree. And fair play to some personalities, including Mr Campbell, they are beginning to get themselves into action. Another success is that three years ago, I received a phone

call from one of the co-ordinators of the Belfast Action Team, and
he asked me could I come down to see him. I brought a local
representative down with me, Hughie Smyth. And he says: 'I've a
quarter million pounds to spend on the Shankill Road, I could do
a little bit of landscaping here and there, but I'm receiving opposition'. He couldn't understand this. I didn't know what the Belfast
Action Team was; however, we knew that it wasn't some kind of
papish plot. So, we said: 'Right, that's OK. Come on ahead'. Those
minions who were political representatives, we said to them: 'We
need this particular development'. We got the Belfast Action
Team in. And as a result of that we have several vehicles, we've
opened the Shankill Development Agency, we have the Shankill
Activity Centre, we have the Shankill Community Council, and we
have other achievements. So, the success story is not yet com-
pleted, but it has taken its first steps to success.

Brian Garrett:
William Campbell, can you supplement that?

William Campbell (Shankill Road Mission, Belfast):
I don't completely agree, obviously, with what Mr Spence said. As
superintendent of the Shankill Mission, on the Lower Shankill,
and a minister of the Presbyterian Church, I'm coming at this
from a different angle. The Shankill Road Mission is there since
1907. A long time before we were having troubles on the Shankill
Road, the Shankill Road Mission was thriving. We were amongst
the people, from the time Henry Montgomery formed the Shankill
Road Mission. And with his very effective way of dealing with
problems, he handed out food, clothing, provided holidays for the
kids to go down to Bangor on the tram, and so on. All this pre-
dated the current situation. We have been responding and react-
ing to people's needs on the Shankill from 1907.

I would agree that the churches *per se* have been backward about
coming forward on the Shankill – possibly because of the way things
got done. We are now an employer, providing employment for sixty-
five folk on an ACE scheme. We have the Shankill Parade Home for
single homeless and those with an alcohol problem, a dry house. We
have it staffed twenty-four hours a day, and we have a full-time
manager in there. We have a drop-in centre, which provides
subsidized meals Monday to Friday, with a games room deliberately
built for the unemployed folk: in other words, they get a game of

snooker or table tennis free, and one good meal a day. We have a facility there for different groups in the community: a mother and toddlers group, a Beacon House club, and so on.

But having said all of that, there's still a need, as far as I see, for us as a mission to be in amongst people and, in partnership with government through the social services, to provide as many facilities as we can. And I would say that that's how I see our work ahead. Not in opposition in any way, but I think that there are a lot of groups who are working, you in your small corner and I in mine; and perhaps there could be a greater degree of co-ordination within the Shankill area, bringing together the clerical groups as well as the straight-up-and-down community groups, so that the work doesn't get too diffuse and get lost somewhere.

Brian Garrett:
I did say I would ask you to say something about your experience in Derry, Eileen.

Eileen Webster (Child Care Social Worker, Derry):
Yes. I'm from West Belfast originally, but I've been a child care social worker with the Western Health and Social Services Board in Derry for sixteen years now. I was struck by the point Joyce McCartan made, about the local voluntary organizations not being identified with the community because members of the community don't feel part of them; they tend not to be on management committees and boards of directors, and therefore those committees aren't seen to be accountable or subject to recall. Obviously, that's absolutely true in the statutory sector, where I work. But it's also true of far too many voluntary organizations, that are of the community, but don't involve the community enough; and therefore this 'them and us' aura is a real barrier.

We're talking about poverty and social disadvantage, and I think we're all guilty of a 'them' and 'us' attitude, no matter how much we yearn for a more equitable distribution of wealth and want to empower the poor. We're all guilty of doing that, because we know best. We're here today because we've a bit of knowledge and a bit of relevant background, in terms of the work that we do. But the actual financial despair, the material despair of poverty, is compounded by that feeling of powerlessness, of being disenfranchised; that even a local community association doesn't particularly involve me – if, for example, I'm a single parent, and I've got four

kids, and I don't feel able, or capable. They don't make me feel
capable enough to be involved in running that local community
association, or tenants' association, or whatever it happens to be.

And I think that that's a real barrier to those who are below the
poverty line being involved in doing something about their own
personal circumstances. Those that are poorest in Derry, as anywhere else, are those least involved in any community action,
because they're in despair; because they're on valium; because
they have alcohol dependency problems, or whatever. All as a
result of their material circumstances, and that's the bottom line.
There are some estates that I work in, like Upper Creggan, Galliagh,
that have upwards of 80% male unemployment. They're totally
disenfranchized from the normal course of community action.

Social workers, of course, have two heads! We never win. Right
through from Maria Colwell in the early 70s, through to the recent
stuff in Orkney, Cleveland, and elsewhere. We either err on the
side of caution and children die and we're to blame, or we are too
zealous and we deprive children of their liberties and deprive
parents of their children, and so on. Social workers as a profession
accept that no-win situation, and try to do the best we can, particularly in the child protection area I work in. Child protection must
mean prevention of children falling into danger at the hands of
whoever; and the statutory agencies and the Government certainly
don't allow us to do the preventative work that I would like to be
involved in.

The under-resourcing and the under-staffing of social work in
Northern Ireland is an on-going battle, because, unlike Britain,
where local authorities have the budgetary responsibility for social
services, and the National Health Service budget is entirely separate, here we have the combined Health and Social Services Boards;
and Personal Social Services are the poor sister, or brother, of the
medical profession – always were and always will be, as long as that
structure remains. Therefore, we're always fighting a continual
battle for resources. So what my colleagues and I in Derry, as I'm
sure is the case in any other area of social work in Northern
Ireland, are doing, is running from one child protection crisis to
another. We're not getting our teeth into the preventative work.

Therefore, on the one hand, disenfranchized and disempowered
people who are in receipt of social security benefits are led to
believe that we are a resource, to enable them to help themselves
out of their despair and out of whatever trough they're in. And on

the other hand, we find ourselves having to go along and explain that we're actually not able to do that. It's a very demoralizing area to be involved in.

I don't know how anyone lives on social security benefits. I don't know how anyone can be expected to make ends meet. I'm not talking about luxuries, like cigarettes (I am a smoker myself), or alcohol or holidays, or two pairs of shoes instead of one for your child, a pair of shoes and a pair of sandals. I'm talking about the basic necessities of life: food, lighting and heat, and a roof over your head. Day and daily, I see that social security benefit levels don't equip anyone to meet those basic needs. And then, a couple of years ago we had the Fowler Review, Norman Fowler's infamous review of social security legislation, which introduced the Social Fund. The previous system of single payments, whereby people could apply for grants for special needs – for clothing, for bedding, for basic furnishings (you were never allowed for carpet, only lino) – was done away with, and the Derry social security offices, with the levels of unemployment in Derry we're all aware of, were allocated less than 40% of the money that had been there previously.

Furthermore, that 40% was to provide loans that had to be repaid to Social Security, as well as one-off grants. So I find that the majority of people that I work with at the moment are well below the official poverty line because of their debt: because they have had loans from Social Security to meet the basic necessities of life, and then have had to repay those loans out of their social security benefits. And worse than that: they've had one loan and they have fifty-two weeks (or in certain exceptional circumstances I think it's a year and a half) to repay the loan. But you know, Christmas comes once a year, and you want to get a few little luxuries or toys for the children, so people fall further into debt. And there's a horrible spate of private loan sharks operating in areas where I work, like Creggan and Shantallow and Ballymagroarty and the Brandywell and the Bogside, so that people are in horrendous debt and worry and despair.

We used to hear years ago, in the horrible tabloid press, about the welfare scroungers going to Majorca for their holidays, etc., but I have yet to meet a person in that kind of debt who isn't desperately worried about it; who isn't heartsick thinking about it day and daily; and can't see further than the next day or the next week, in terms of that grinding debt. Not just grinding poverty, but grinding debt. Therefore, the view of the social worker – such as myself or any statutory agency, or any voluntary agency – being able to alleviate that poverty and that debt just isn't there among those poor people in the Derry area. And I don't think it's any different anywhere else.

I just want to make one very small point about the physical make-up of Derry. As you probably know, on the west bank the vast majority of the population are Catholic, and on the east bank they're Protestant. When you have that grinding poverty, and you don't have holidays, and you don't even go to the other side of the city to Lisnagelvin Sports Centre to go swimming, for instance, because if you live on the east bank you don't have the bus fare, then the sectarian divide is so real, for children and adults alike. And the mythology is so real: that we in Creggan are so poor here and everybody's on benefits and we have 80% unemployment – and that somehow it's different on Irish Street, just the other side of the River Foyle. Of course it's not, no more than it's very much different on the Shankill than on the Falls. But that perception, because of the grinding poverty, can't be eradicated.

You can't get round that, you can't convince people that the unemployment or the poverty in Irish Street is the same, or that the social security recipients are in the same position. It's an impossible task. Voluntary schemes like Holiday Projects West, who take kids away for a week or two in the summer from both sections of the community, and the little lad from Irish Street goes home wearing a tricolour that the wee boy from the Bogside gave him, and they meet every three months for a disco – they're absolutely meaningless. I'm sorry I have to say that, but they don't in any way break down any of the sectarian barriers. And that's something that poverty does as well. And I think that **is** the bottom line. It's not security and the other issues that Tom Hadden was emphasizing; and I would take exception to those points that he made.

Anne Sloan (Director, Forum for Community Work Education):
Having listened to the last speaker, Brian, I am wondering whether what we do really makes any difference. Basically, we seek to promote community work in Northern Ireland through education and training. We run a number of courses which are based on the work which community groups are doing in their own communities, such as environmental work, community care, and whatever. I

was very conscious of that when you were talking this morning, Roisín, about people being able to actually take part in management and being able to tackle their own problems. We try to run our courses in a way that actually involves people in helping to run things, so that they have a real role in it, because we think it's important to instil confidence in them.

But alongside the confidence, we need knowledge; because we believe that knowledge is power. There are so many people living in estates, and they actually don't know how the system works. They don't know how to tackle an issue. But they can become aware of how the system works, become confident about their own ability. And it's my opinion that people can actually do any of the things that you were talking about. And you know that too. If they can get that confidence, they can then define the issues themselves, and they know where to go and how to tackle them. Perhaps that is one thing (I'm not saying it's the be-all-and-end-all) that does get through to government sometimes. If they get seventeen letters from people in a local area, all more or less saying the same thing, all obviously from residents in that area – as somebody said, it can be like the road to Damascus. Sometimes that will get across, and they can effect change. At least, that's what I hope and believe.

I know the benefits are inadequate. I know that what we're doing doesn't tackle that problem. On the other hand, it means that those people are coming together, and they're meeting each other, and they're realizing that they're not stupid, that they can do things. So therefore, they're realizing themselves, without being in any way underdogs, that they are in poverty, but they can develop a kind of pride in their own achievement and in their own neighbourhood. That's the sort of thing we're trying to do. We're trying to give people knowledge, because we think knowledge is power. We're trying to help them develop their self-confidence, so that they can use the knowledge that they've got themselves to proper effect. And we're also saying that people should be able to tackle their own issues in their own areas. I'd say we're working very well, at a basic level. But I can't answer the question: does it make any difference?

Brian Garrett:
Could I then take up another strand. We have here today senior representatives of probably the two best-known bodies in the voluntary sector: the Northern Ireland Council for Voluntary

Action and the Northern Ireland Voluntary Trust. For those who don't come from Northern Ireland, they embrace the whole of the Province, they intend not to be sectional – that is to say, not to work exclusively in any particular area. Seamus, could you tell us a little bit about the work of the Northern Ireland Council for Voluntary Action?

Seamus McAleavey (Assistant Director, Northern Ireland Council for Voluntary Action):
NICVA was founded in 1938, as the Northern Ireland Council for Social Services. We are on the support and advice side. We're sort of an umbrella organization. In the past, we would've been seen as a liberal unionist-type organization that would have dealt with large voluntary groups. As part of trying to change our image, we've changed our name to the Northern Ireland Council for Voluntary Action. We see ourselves as promoting community development, and we're an organization that is committed to social change. We try to promote activities within the voluntary sector. We now encompass community organizations which are based on the ground, in local regions or districts.

There is a tension within the voluntary sector between the bigger voluntary organizations, which are Northern Ireland wide, and those which are on the ground in local areas. We try to ride both those horses. We administer the Give-As-You-Earn scheme and the Cheques for Charity scheme, which are tax-efficient methods of giving to charities. But we also provide training facilities for other voluntary and community groups. We are really trying to promote community development. Gusty Spence was saying earlier that work was going on in Protestant areas. Some of our staff have been involved in recent work in community development in Protestant areas. It's a question of trying to network groups, so that people learn from others' experiences, and we don't all have to reinvent the wheel every time.

Brian Garrett:
Could I ask Paul Sweeney, of the Northern Ireland Voluntary Trust, to tell us a little bit about your work.

Paul Sweeney (Director, Northern Ireland Voluntary Trust):
First of all, I feel a bit like Anne, in some respects, in trying to follow what Roisín said this morning, and more immediately what

Eileen has said. I'm still tingling from both those presentations. The Northern Ireland Voluntary Trust is a charitable trust. We were set up in 1979, and we do two main things. One, we give out grants to self-help community projects throughout Northern Ireland, to local groups who are starting off and, as Anne said, trying to express and trying to meet their own needs. The other side of the coin is that we actually raise money to enable us to do this. We raise money mainly in England, and we now have a capital sum of £4 million, which is, if you like, a community chest, owned by the people of Northern Ireland. The current eleven trustees have custodianship of that. Our aim is to build up a community chest of about five or six million pounds, that would be there in perpetuity. We work off the income from that each year, and the trustees employ a small number of staff whose role is to receive applications from local groups, appraise the groups, and recommend groups for grants.

In working for the NIVT, it does give us some kind of pan-Northern Ireland experience, and we do see our work as part of some kind of anti-poverty strategy. But, there's no question about it, it's becoming increasingly difficult – for the reasons that Roisín and Eileen spoke of – to engage local people and expect of them skills and resources and energy. It simply wouldn't be expected of an affluent section of our population, so I think it's more and more difficult to keep hope alive in the circumstances that Eileen spoke of.

In terms of our other role, we try to have some input to government, because we have a pan-Northern Ireland role. We try to analyse our experiences and feed some views into government. I actually think it's a very important time to be alive in Northern Ireland in terms of poverty, because poverty raises questions about affluence as well; and what concerns me is the level of indifference in Northern Ireland towards the issues that we're talking about. The kind of messages that Roisín and Eileen have been giving this morning aren't heard, because people are indifferent or ambivalent – because, for the most part, Northern Ireland is working well. Northern Ireland is working, and we have a tremendous amount of affluence here.

Gusty was talking about the 11-plus failures on the Shankill Road. The reason why we have an education system that creates poverty, that creates failures, is because we will it. We will that system. The 11-plus system works extremely well. It churns out some of the greatest kids in the United Kingdom; and particularly in the Protestant community, those kids then get out. So we have almost a corrupt educational crisis. We're creating a lot of failures at one end, and we're creating some successes at the other end, so that the natural commercial and civic and political leadership can get out.

Tom Hadden says: 'This place is in a mess'. I actually do think that Northern Ireland is in a mess. But it's small enough. If we had the will to do something about it, you could actually set some very clear targets here for the next ten to twenty years. You could engage people like this, in the kind of strategy that Roisín was talking about, and actually effect some positive change. Indeed, that would be the hidden agenda of the NIVT: to create opportunities for debate and challenge. And I think that it's interesting the way that the state, at least the ten permanent secretaries here, are becoming more and more sensitized to the crises in our local communities, and the need to develop a coherent strategy.

And that's why I want to congratulate the organizers today, the Irish Association, for getting people together. We must first of all engage the intelligentsia, because the intellectual debate about poverty, and the need to tackle it, has got to be won first. We've got to get the opinion leaders. We've got to create a climate in which we understand that we're paying an enormous price here for the poverty that we have; and that if we remain indifferent towards it, it affects the quality of all our lives. And yet, it's something we could do something about if the will was created. But we must create a climate in which poverty is raised up the agenda.

Michael Brown (The Irish Association):
When I became a Belfast city councillor in 1973, in East Belfast there were something like 30,000 houses which were unfit for people to live in. I remember a girl who had a very nice job in the Central Library coming home every night to a house with one bedroom, no kitchen, a sort of living-room with a sink, a tap the other side of the yard, and an outside loo. Those were typical conditions. This kind of thing was all over the North of Ireland. Often the country was worse off than the cities.

I worked in Rathgael Training School for fourteen years, and there we had the experience of having no support whatsoever from our civil servant masters. I gather that that has now completely changed. But it took twelve or fourteen years to get it done. We worked there in spite of civil servants. Northern Ireland is changing, but it is changing desperately slowly. I quite agree that we now have the politicians that we deserve. We put them in place ourselves. What we've got to learn is that lesson, and try and get politicians who help people.

Constance Short:
I just want to say something about the broad picture. All these things that people have been saying are valid. But I don't think there should be any despair, because really the fact that the Irish Association are having this thing here today is a perfect reflection of the fact that all of us realize that it's absolutely essential that people on the ground control their own situation, and that we must set up forums where they can do that. I was at a meeting in Headford, County Galway, recently, setting up a federation of women's groups in Connaught, and it was incredible. *Mná na hÉireann* were there to a woman. The Catholic Church controls a lot of social services and all sorts of things in the Republic – like education groups, drop-in centres, and so on. And one woman stood up and said: 'This is all very grand. It's fine if people show people, as long as they have the wit to leave when the time comes for them to leave'.

And I think that's really the kernel of the whole situation. Everybody knows that we all need educational structures, we need all sorts of advice bureaux and all the rest of it. People on the ground should be encouraged to develop their own situation, but the advisers should have the wit to leave when they're not needed any more. Co-operation North, in the last couple of years, has developed a community programme precisely because they've realized this. And it's not confined to here. When we were all children, we gave money to the black babies; now we're teaching the black babies to feed themselves. Not simply in Northern Ireland, but all over the world, people are realizing more and more that they can control their own situation, at all levels. Society in general realizes that people, simply because they're poor, are not stupid; that education and brain levels and everything else do not belong to a particular class. I think there could be more equality in the world, but this is a beginning. I wouldn't despair.

John Watson (Chairman, Pax Christi, Belfast):
Pax Christi is a peace and reconciliation group, working across the community. As such, we wouldn't be directly involved in the area

of poverty, but very much in the area of discrimination. Just recently we have been looking at the whole question of the association between poverty in the community and the families of people who are in prison. Pax Christi have identified a number of problems there, where ex-prisoners and the families of prisoners are in very many ways disadvantaged. For example, one of the things we've been asked to look at is the relation between churches and prisoners' families. The churches have been doing very little to help such families, much less than the statutory bodies. The churches have branded those families and have disassociated themselves, distanced themselves, rather than bringing them community support.

One of the other things that came up in our recent discussion was the fact that the churches seem to have 'safe' groups, and that the authorities seem to want to put money into safe groups, trusted groups such as churches, and take money away from other established groups that are not church-based, or are in fact 'liberal' and maybe a wee bit antagonistic towards the churches. There's consolidation there of the power structures. In the churches, for example (certainly in the Catholic Church), the clergy control the funds, control decision-making, and there's only lip-service to the role of the community. That's been extended by the authorities, when they give their money and put their trust and put power into the hands of the church. They're extending their very tight control, very much male-dominated control; and the community is losing out enormously in that.

One other factor we were asked to look at was the question of education. The general feeling is that quite a number of people have dropped out of education because of the inadequacies of the education system, and that we need to re-establish an alternative education for adults in the community, most especially those who feel that they've been disadvantaged, in many ways, and would like a sheltered type of educational surrounding where they can feel at home, do not feel embarrassed, and can begin to promote their own self-awareness and their own education.

Brian Garrett:
Joyce McCartan, I want to come back to the point you were raising earlier, that is, the problem of getting a representative body. You're from the Women's Information Drop-in Centre on the Lower Ormeau Road in Belfast. How successful were you in Lower Ormeau?

Joyce McCartan:
Very successful.

Brian Garrett:
How did you do that?

Joyce McCartan:
By getting the people involved. When people are in control of their own lives and doing their own things, they take more pride in it. I'm glad to hear you say that, John, about the churches, where they take control. You know, people in the community know what they need, and it's up to them to have control of their own lives and do their own things, and not have people dictating to them what they think's good for them. In the Lower Ormeau Road, we set up a Women's Drop-in Centre in 1987; and with women coming in, we realized the need and the poverty in the area, and we decided to do something about it. So, we all got together, and when the building next door went idle we decided to buy it. So we raised money from different trusts over in England to pay for it, and from the Belfast Action Team. Luckily enough, we had somebody who believed we could do it. There was a lot of people said: 'Oh, these are women – they'll not be able to do anything to get it off the ground'. But we've proved ourselves. We have set up Mornington Enterprises, which is controlled by the people in the community that are on the board.

Brian Garrett:
How do you elect your people? You don't have an election of all of the district, do you?

Joyce McCartan:
I'm going to tell you something! When you look round the community, you see a lot of people there with talent.

Brian Garrett:
But how do you get genuinely representative bodies?

Joyce McCartan:
People that are interested in it, and see the need within the community, come together and start working and build it up. That's how we did it. We've worked hard together, and we've

created work in the community. I see that as a need in all communities, because no way are big factories going to come back into Northern Ireland again. And I think it's up to the people in the community to look round their own community, see what need there is there, see how much work it will create, and start building on that. Because we are looking to the future. We are hoping to become self-supportive. And I think that's what all the people in communities need to do, to try and bring a bit of money into the community and to build up the community. You know, all over the years it's been the poor that've made the rich richer. And I think it's about time that the poor made themselves a wee bit better off, with a decent standard of living and more money coming into the home, and a better education for the children. Those are the things that we are fighting for on the Lower Ormeau Road.

Brian Garrett:
There are two or three members of the Committee for the Administration of Justice here. One of the things we should all know is that the CAJ recently published a handbook which was designed to assist people to know their rights. Would somebody like to say a little bit about what the CAJ is doing at the minute in relation to social welfare issues, as opposed to other legal issues.

Paul Noonan (Committee on the Administration of Justice, Sub-Committee on Racism):
Well, my colleague and I have been working with the CAJ sub-group dealing with racism, and I'd like to address that issue. I work for the Northern Ireland Council for Travelling People. This conference is about various forms of discrimination, yet I notice that the group against whom discrimination has been practised for at least as long as religious discrimination has been practised in Northern Ireland was omitted from the programme of today's seminar. For example, there's documentary evidence that under Elizabeth the First, the death penalty was introduced for being a gypsy. Nowadays, the death penalty as such isn't formalized for travelling people, but I would argue that discrimination is still very much a fact of life.

It's a structural discrimination. It's a discrimination which denies travelling people access to a decent place to live, which in turn forces them to live in roadside camps, without access to toilets, running water, electricity supply, hard standing, and any decent facilities. This takes a very heavy toll on travelling people. It means that the infant mortality rate is three times that of the settled community. It means that the average life expectancy is fifty years of age. It's also meant that only 10% of the travelling community are literate. These are very serious measures of social deprivation. No travellers in Northern Ireland have ever gone on to third-level education. I would agree very much with the points made by Roisín in her speech, that it's structural discrimination which needs to be addressed, and accessing the whole range of services to travellers; as well as the outright repression which has been adopted against travellers. And that is still very much evident in the number of evictions that some of you may have read about in the papers over the last week here in Belfast.

The other approach that has been adopted has been one of manipulative paternalism, where travelling people are seen as having a culture which is deviant: in particular, the nomadic element of their culture, where travellers move from place to place – they travel. You had a series of voluntary committees, which used to be known as itinerant resettlement committees, despite the fact that the word 'itinerant' itself is offensive to travellers. The aim of these committees was to try and settle travellers in houses, civilize them, knock the rough edges off them, and generally take a missionary approach towards travellers.

We would argue very much that the issue isn't just simply one of poverty – although we would accept the wider definition of poverty, in terms of lack of recognition of culture, access to services, and so on. It's not just simply material poverty. There's a small minority of travellers who are quite wealthy; there are other travellers who are extremely poor. So, we would argue that the issue at stake as regards travelling people is the fact that they're not accepted as a distinct ethnic group.

We would argue that they are an ethnic group, for a number of criteria that anthropologists put forward, such as endogamy, a shared history and life-style and customs, the fact that the travellers have their own secret language, and so on. It's the racism which denies travellers expression of their ethnicity which is the problem that should be addressed, rather than just treating the symptoms of the problem. It has been suggested, in the 1990 Report of the Standing Advisory Commission on Human Rights, that travellers should be specifically mentioned in the Race Relations Act and that it should be extended to Northern Ireland. This would provide a bedrock, or a basis, for addressing all the other areas, all the symptoms, that we talked about – infant mortality, access to health provision, access to education, and so on.

Brian Garrett:
It's only fair to mention that the Irish Association did have a special one-day conference devoted entirely to the problems experienced by travelling people, last December in Dublin; and that the Irish Association has sponsored the President Robinson Awards for the Design of Travellers' Accommodation.

William Campbell:
Could I ask a question, to do with the education part of it? By the very nature of being a traveller, and with the system of education which pertains in both parts of the island, how do you envisage educating the children of travellers? I've got kids, and they've got to go to school every day, Monday to Friday. I'm not taking issue with anything you said. Just how do you deal with the children's education?

Paul Noonan:
Well, it's a very complex answer to your question. First of all, I might say that I don't think travelling children want education. They are educated by their parents. They are educated in their own life-style, in their own way of life. But as regards formal education, I think that travellers are excluded from the sort of first-class service that should be offered. The school, for instance, that travelling children attend in Belfast is located in a slum school building, that's overcrowded, with no playground. The children are given a special curriculum, and access for children to attend mainstream schools is made very difficult. Often, principals of other schools are approached by the parents of travelling children, and they're told there's a special school for travellers in Belfast. A special school from which no child has ever got the 11-plus.

Brian Garrett:
Roughly how many people in Northern Ireland would come within this group?

Paul Noonan:
We're talking of about 1,500.

Michael Brown:
Everybody who has spoken has mentioned education in one form
or another. This is very important. Again, my experience in the
Rathgael Training School, where I worked, was that all the children coming to us, almost without exception, were very disturbed,
and most of them could hardly read and couldn't write their
names. We ran a school where we had perhaps four or six children
to a teacher, and it was quite extraordinary the results that came
out of it. Because, for the first time in their lives, something had
been made interesting for them, and because they were getting
personal attention. So many of these children get into the back
row of a classroom and are just not interested, and that's that. This
is very relevant in the case of the travellers. Somehow or other, the
education world is going to have to be pushed into realizing that
children cannot do well in classes of thirty or forty.

Brian Garrett:
This first session has been really to identify who we are. If you
agree, I thought we might, after lunch, come to the 'what should
now be done' issue; and secondly, the issue of how these problems
impact upon the attitude of the communities to each other. It
seems to me those are the two big issues. We all remember different things from Roisín's talk. But the first thing I remember about
it was the danger of having a community development 'industry'
which is not in fact dealing with the issues which underlie it. Then,
when the issue came up of the danger of just working with activists,
that's why I took up with Joyce McCartan the question as to how
you actually go about getting a representative body. And the third
thing which I remember, Roisín, was that you actually identified a
single priority, which was the need for facilities for mothers, for
play centres. You suggested that that might strike at the very heart
of their inability to get education, jobs, or whatever.

There is a proliferation of community organizations. And for
those of us who aren't in them, it's difficult to know what should
be done, what should be the practical priorities of the region to
deal with the problems we have identified. The second question I
thought we might look at in the next session is, whether or not the
type of community development which has happened in Northern
Ireland has in fact reinforced the divisions rather than dissolved
them. Are the community organizations guilty on occasion of
reinforcing the divisions between Catholics and Protestants, and

by highlighting grievance as such not getting to grips with the
sense of deprivation?

[Editor's note: Unfortunately, due to a technical problem, the
proceedings of the afternoon session of this workshop were not
recorded.]

DISCRIMINATION AGAINST WOMEN

Tess Hurson (Fortnight Educational Trust):
What I thought we might do this morning is air some of the issues that you feel are relevant to the topic of discrimination against women; and then this afternoon draw together some recommendations about how some of the particular issues could be addressed.

Perhaps the obvious question (which underneath may not be all that obvious) is: 'Is there discrimination against women in Northern Ireland, or indeed, in Ireland generally?' If there is discrimination, why are women discriminated against? Is their position in society worse now than it was a hundred years ago? I think we need to start thinking about some of the root causes of it, in the same way as Roisín talked about the root causes of disadvantage and poverty. If it exists, what measures can women, or women working with men, use to ameliorate or get rid of discrimination? Another major question that might be asked is: 'What is the relationship between discrimination and stereotyping?'

Now, it struck me that there might be various areas in which discrimination may be occurring. One is the economic field; and we may want to ask ourselves: where do areas of discrimination lie within the economic field? For example, do they lie in career prospects, in wage levels, in the area of training and education, or in the interface between career and other kinds of things, like family life? To put it another way: does discrimination cause social and psychological conflicts? Do the problems lie in the area of jobs and perceptions, which brings us back to the idea of stereotypes again?

Another big issue, in terms of discrimination, is women and sexuality. That would take in areas like contraception, divorce and separation, rape and abuse, and role stereotypes within relationships: for example, who pays when you go to the cinema? There

are other areas: for example, women in politics. Within the Northern Ireland context, are women discriminated against as a sub-
group within wider discriminations? Are there class differences in
discrimination against women? Further issues include women and
violence (which takes in both political violence and domestic and
other forms of violence). Are women discriminated against in the
arts?

There's also the 'mammy phenomenon', as I call it, whereby
mothers can unwittingly contribute to discrimination against themselves. Are there differences in the experience of discrimination
between women in urban contexts and women living outside big
cities like Belfast and Derry? Are there discriminations in the
relationship of women to religion? Is there discrimination in areas
like women in health, women and disablement, and one that maybe
cuts across quite a few of those issues, women as carers? That is my
proposed list of some of the things that we might want to talk about.
I'd like now to turn it over to you and get your responses, and
perhaps add other topics that we might want to talk about.

**Mina Wardle (Shankill Stress, Agoraphobia, and Prescribed Drugs
Abuse Group, Belfast):**
I'm the co-ordinator of the Shankill Stress and Agoraphobia Group,
which incidentally covers the Falls and Andersonstown as well.
'Shankill' is in the title just because that's where the idea was
conceived. All the hundred and twenty people that I look after are
women, and all the people who work for me are women. If you
would like, we could start off by talking about the forms of discrimination suffered by the women in my group.

First of all, the area I work in is in West Belfast, so we have
discrimination right away, which doesn't just affect one part of
West Belfast or the other, it affects the whole of West Belfast.
Politically, we're disenfranchized: we don't have a representative
in Westminster, or in Dublin – and Euro-MPs are known not to
come into the district. So anything that we do is without the help
that an MP from the area could give us. It does have a very bad
impact on the women; it seems that the women have always shoul-
dered the responsibility in that area. So we find that that is a
terrible disadvantage, and I don't know how we can address that
problem at all.

We are particularly worried about carers, and there is definitely
discrimination against women carers. Someone who's had to give

up a career to look after a mother or a father, for example, and is out for a long time, can't get back into that career again. They suffer great financial loss. They suffer loss of identity. They suffer everything, but most of it is financial. And there is no help available for these women at all, there's no one to advise them. Nobody seems to care and nobody seems to want to do anything about it. You're a woman, and it's your responsibility to look after your parent. In the mental health section of our area, there is definitely discrimination which the women didn't even realize was there. People who had breakdowns in various post-trauma situations discovered that they had a mental health record, which now has to be declared. Therefore, if they're applying for a job, they're discriminated against; and if they go for a job promotion they might lose their jobs. I can only speak for women, because I only deal with women; but definitely something needs to be done about that.

The family life situation, again in that area, is maybe peculiar to working-class areas; but women are still fighting their way out of a system where the husband is the boss of the house, and the woman is the mother, and the parent, and the wife, and whatever else she has to be. We still have women in the group, believe it or not, who have to ask can they have a night out to go to a meeting, who have to say what time they'll be home at – and very often they have to leave a number they can be phoned at, in case one of the children wakens during that time.

Religious discrimination – yes, there is discrimination against women in the churches. As in politics, they're allowed quite a lot of responsibility, and no authority at all. In terms of education, there are classes they can go to, but they have no crèche, and they can't afford to pay babysitters. So, there is discrimination against women in further education.

Economically, the burden is on women as well. Particularly, we have a terrible problem with loan sharks; and the men just walk off and the women are left with the responsibility in this very dangerous area. In divorce, I know there is discrimination against some men, but the women are terribly discriminated against, even though they were perhaps not to blame for the divorce. In disablement as well, there is the problem of discrimination: a woman going to see a psychiatrist or going to see a doctor very, very often doesn't get the help she needs, until her husband actually stamps his feet at these people, and then something is done. Now, I think that's a very sad situation, because it's the women who are suffering.

Tess Hurson:

I think you have touched some very important bases and got right
into the heart of it, Mina. A word that you repeated several times
was the word 'responsibility', and it seems that there's a sense in
which women are expected to do certain things – which brings us
back to what I talked about earlier in terms of stereotypes and the
relationship between discrimination and stereotypes, or clichs, if
you want to use that term. Because certain stereotypes have developed about what women are supposed to do, and in fact what
women are, certain types of discrimination follow on from that, in
terms of the kinds of roles that they find themselves in.

Dominica McGowan (Rape and Incest Line, Belfast):

It occurred to me when you were throwing out your headings that
all those headings were very much interlinked. When I'm talking
about jobs, I'm talking about day care; when I'm talking about day
care, I'm talking about money; and so on. It's hard to know where
to start. When I hear the argument about day care, I think to
myself: 'Why should day care be the responsibility of women?' I
was at a meeting recently, a big discussion between the Boards
about day care, and men weren't mentioned at all. I appreciate
that in real life, ninety-nine percent of women are looking after
children. But there is this assumption that runs through the discussion: 'Well, that's the way it should be'. There is this assumption that women should do, be, act, in a certain way; and also a
long agenda of what they shouldn't do. They automatically should
be carers; they should be looking after children; they shouldn't
have power; they shouldn't query the status quo.

It's almost like what Roisín was saying about the difference
between feeding the poor and asking why the poor are hungry.
When you query why women don't have power, then you're la-
belled as a feminist, or a radical, or an extremist, or you're talking
gibberish. So it's OK to offer some recommendations about how
to provide day care, but it's not OK to query the whole power issue
surrounding that. I'm not suggesting that I have an answer. I
suppose, if you ask a question, you should have some idea of the
answer. I don't have any idea of the answer; but it's just to question
the whole assumptions that underlie the issue.

Tess Hurson:

I suspect that what you're saying might also be identified by people in other workshops as a similar phenomenon, that there's a sense in which there's a safe set of things that can be said, and after that what you're into is a sort of negative labelling of one sort or another. It'll be interesting to see whether or not that actually emerges from some of the other workshops, and whether that's a thing that's inherent in the whole phenomenon of discrimination.

Joan McKiernan (Centre for Research on Women, University of Ulster):
Could I just make a point about the way in which the workshops have been organized? In every facet of life there is oppression of women. But yet, the question of women is shunted into one workshop. Everything that is being discussed in those other workshops, we should be able to raise how it affects women – whether it's poverty, employment, emergency legislation. We could go on endlessly talking about the areas in which women are discriminated against. But I think it would be more important to be there, raising the issues in the general body. That's why I want to get back to the point about power.

Obviously, the question of power comes up no matter what the context is. And the question of the appropriate challenges to the existing power structure is based on certain assumptions. But when you talk about needs, you raise the whole question of the social welfare system, which is all very much based on the needs of men, and the idea that everybody lives in a proper happy family, where there are no single parents, no separated women, no women choosing to live alone. There are so many women women with families, women without families – who are all being discriminated against, because they're not being treated as individuals, because they're not living in the right kind of a traditional arrangement. Besides the fact that the payments are all too low, women are treated in terms of whether they are a wife, an ex-wife, about to be a wife. Another area is the whole question of reproductive rights, especially the right to abortion. It's a whole load of things that need to be discussed, it's every part of society.

Tess Hurson:
I think your point is well taken. Ultimately, it's a chicken and egg situation. I think what's coming out from Dominica as well, and from Mina, is the interlinked and interrelated nature of discrimination as it exists.

Patricia Feeney:
It's also important not to do nothing until you have all that you want.
I think that we should do something about the things that we can do
something about, we should do something about the most obvious
injustices and build on those whilst we're waiting for Utopia; in the
meantime, we can start, for example, to make sure that the carers
are paid enough, or that there should be some concept of career
break. Because, in most of those situations, unfortunately, the
caring situation is limited, because the sick person is going to die,
so there should be a concept of a career break.

There are many, many things that can be done to deal with the
most obvious discriminations. For example, the question of who is
the tenant of the house: when the family breaks up, the wife may
find herself left with the children, but her husband has the ten-
ancy of the house. There are many very obvious things, and I think
it's those kinds of things that politically we should be addressing
(and you were talking, Mina, about not having political representation). There should be ways in which all of those things are
listed, at a very primitive level to begin with.

Of course, alongside that, we should be addressing the problem
of stereotyping. I'm a teacher, and I think that the basic way in
which that has to be done is through education, and not just in
girls' schools but in boys' schools, and I think there's an enormous
weight of society to be shifted or moved slightly, but that's such an
enormous task. One thing did strike home to me very much: I deal
with adolescent girls all the time, and the issue of health care is
one which I get steamed up about very often, because there are
girls who are having quite severe menstrual problems at that stage
of their lives. Disabling, in many, many cases. And their mothers
take them to the doctor, and I recommend that their mothers take
them back again and again; and the only response from the doctor
is: 'Ach, she'll grow out of it'. Or: 'She'll be OK when she has
babies'. But, of course, that's from a man who doesn't understand
what it's going to be like for that girl for the ten years it may take
her.

I'm not making it up, because it happens to the girls that I work
with, day in and day out. It is symptomatic of the attitudes of
society to women, of the low value that is put on their health, and
the low value that is put on their well-being, and the fact that it
isn't that important, because, in any case, at that stage in her life
she's not working, and she's not taking days off work. The fact that

she may be taking days off school, and in the end is less capable of getting a job simply because her attainments are low because of absenteeism – none of that's considered.

There are things that can be done immediately to deal with those problems; and, at the same time, the whole of society, the whole education system should be taking on board the whole issue of discrimination.

Tess Hurson:

I want to ask just one question before we go any further. Are there any of you who feel that women are not discriminated against?

Lila Knox (The Irish Association):

I don't think I feel I've ever felt discriminated against; but there's one thing I'd like to say. We've talked about society stereotyping women. Who is this society? It's **women**, as much as men.

Maureen Alden (The Queen's University of Belfast):

This idea of women stereotyping women is very true. It took me years to find out. I was not married at the time. I had no children. I still have no children. I kept finding myself in situations where all the interest of the women seemed to be in marriage, and they began to compete with one another in the number of their children, especially what their children were doing, especially their male children. And it took me years to understand that I was being put in my place, and that this was a competition. It also took me years to understand that the Irish nearly always consider the unmarried as children. I am not suggesting that anyone here would necessarily hold those views, but they have been quite widespread. I know someone who was trying to collect oral history, and some old gentlemen would not tell their accounts to unmarried women, but only to married women, because an unmarried woman was not a proper recipient for the recollections of these old gentlemen.

Joan McKiernan:

Lots of very confident women feel that way, because they have done well in life. But that doesn't say anything about the mass of women. There **is** discrimination against women. Just because you, personally, have never felt discriminated against, that doesn't say anything about the mass of women. And if we look at women's place in society, if we look at how much money women make, if we

look at how many women don't go to work because they've got to
stay home and look after the kids – that's the facts of life. It's not
because women have bad attitudes.

All people have bad attitudes, it's a sexist society. We all grow up
in it, we learn things from our parents. And if you are a good
parent and try and rear non-sexist children, just try it. By the time
they're four and they're going out to play with other kids in the
street, or they start going to nursery school and start learning
roles, and you have other teachers teaching them how to behave,
and you have television – it is very difficult to counteract stereotypes in society. So society has it all wrapped up. And then you go
to get a job, and it continues in terms of the barriers that are raised
against women. So we can't blame women for the kinds of attitudes that they pass on to their kids. They get it from outside.

Lila Knox:
I don't think it's a question of blaming. I think it's a question of
accepting responsibility; and women have to accept the responsibility of changing their position, because no one else is going to do it.

John Fisher (Northern Ireland Office):
What you're saying, Maureen, is that there's not only discrimination against women by men and perhaps by society in general, but
also discrimination against groups of women by other groups of
women – which had not really occurred to me before.

Maureen Alden:
What I'm trying to say is, perhaps there are underlying assumptions that have been unconsciously fostered; and that does lead to
discrimination against some groups of women by other women,
and patronizing attitudes.

Mina Wardle:
I think I know exactly what you're saying. You were saying, Maureen,
about family attitudes to unmarried women. Maybe it's typical of
Belfast, but in my family, even married women are treated as
children. My mother would still see me as a ten-year-old irresponsible person, because I don't impress the values on my children that
she would have impressed on me. I could still feel that way in a
family situation, although I'm a married woman, especially with a
very domineering parent.

Dominica McGowan:
What discrimination to me is about is not achieving or getting your rights, or whatever you want to call it, because of your sex. I think child-care should be available as a right of children. It should be a child's right to have a place in a child-care facility, if parents want it – both male and female. It's their responsibility to do whatever they think is appropriate for the child, but I don't think it should be the responsibility of women to make sure there are child-care facilities.

I agree with what you said, Patricia, but I didn't agree with your use of the word 'Utopian'. When you use a word like 'idealistic' or 'Utopian', it pushes the goal so far ahead you can't see it, you think it's unrealistic and you're never going to achieve it. I also agree that if you want to go a long way, you start by taking small steps. You get your child-care facilities and you get your jobs. I don't think you should stop and wait until you get where you want to be. It should be a mixture of both. You shouldn't simply be working on the small steps and forget about where you want to end up.

Una O'Higgins O'Malley (The Irish Association):
I just want to go back to your question: does everybody here agree that there's discrimination against women? I certainly do, and I think the discriminations against women are very scvere, and I would like to say that they get more severe as women get older, with what I call the 'little old lady' syndrome, which even we ourselves talk about. It catches up with us all in the end.

I do also think that there is discrimination against men. I don't know as much about it as I do about discrimination against women. I don't feel it in my gut to the same extent, but I know it's there; and I see it, curiously enough, more particularly in my married sons, who (I'm thankful to say) are doing shared parenting jobs with their children. One of them, who delivers the two babies every day to the day-care centre and collects them, feels that the women who run the cr che, and run it very well, don't really share with him the day's events of that baby in the way they would if it was mamma was collecting them. He feels that they kind of treat him like a second-class parent, and that if it was his wife who was there she would get more of the story. I don't know whether this is true or not. He certainly feels it.

Then I've gone shopping with another son, who has his little fellow up on the seat of the shopping trolley. He drew my attention to it.

Very often it's a woman who will cut in front of him or push him aside. He isn't considered in quite the same way as a truly caring parent. I think women need an awful lot of support in the alleviation of their problems, all the support they can get; but it would be a pity if they didn't also realize there are serious difficulties for men also.

Dympna McGlade (Ardoyne Women's Research Group, Belfast):
I find the opposite. I work in the community centre in Ardoyne in North Belfast. Women are, generally speaking, the carers. But if a man does the shopping, or minds the child, or whatever, he's wonderful! The women themselves in the centre have come together to do a research project into the needs of women in the area. I don't know where to start talking about discrimination against them. It starts from all ages, all walks of life. We're going to have to come up with some recommendations at the end of the research project, and the recommendations will have to go very far afield – they'll have to deal with the home, the workplace, the Government, education, across the board. It's the way women live their lives and how that's affected them. They're discriminated against from day one, right throughout their lives, and it has got steadily worse, it's not improving.

Joan McKiernan:
That's also because of their class disadvantage. And that's why it's wrong to separate them out and just talk about women's needs. Certainly, all working-class areas will have quite different kinds of problems. That's why I was challenging you about what you said about women discriminating against women. We've had a government headed by Margaret Thatcher, who is a woman. The result of that has been mass discrimination against women. Women are dying on account of health service cuts. Social welfare benefits don't bring food into a house. That's real discrimination, people being deprived of healthy lives.

John Fisher:
What you said about these fantastic men doing the shopping and looking after the kids, that's another example of stereotyping. Stereotyping also works against men. For instance, in the custody and care of children. There is an assumption in the courts that men really can't look after children; and irrespective of the back-

ground of the woman, custody of the children is removed from the man. There are a lot of instances where stereotyping works against men.

Dominica McGowan:
But I wonder is that not based on the majority of cases where women have been the carers earlier on, and the men will want to go off to work anyway, so the court tries to consider how big a break it would be to give control to the father. And certainly, in many cases (I'm not sure of the legalities of it), women may get day-to-day care and control of the child, but very often the man is given the next level of custody, where major decisions in the child's life are made.

Dympna McGlade:
I can only talk about the experience of married women in Ardoyne. The tendency is for couples to get divorced younger and younger. What the men are doing is, they're getting access to the children, taking them for the weekend, and dumping them on the grandparents. They take them to the grandparents on Friday night, pick them up on a Sunday morning, and take them out to the park or whatever.

Mina Wardle:
We seem to be getting bogged down with this one-parent children problem. And I don't think that's what discrimination is all about. It's part of it, it's not all of it.

Tess Hurson:
Your point is taken. I wanted to move on and ask another question, and I ask it of the women here as well as the men. I don't think it's necessarily just a theoretical question at all. In the last ten or twenty years, let's say, has it become any easier for men to begin to assume a fuller parenting role, or are there other factors that are militating against that?

Patricia Feeney:
Could I just say that I really don't think I want to talk about discrimination against men in that one small area, when overwhelmingly in society, discriminations are against women. And I really do not think that we should bend over backwards to

consider the feelings of men in one tiny area of the whole of life, where there's only one small group of men who actually might want custody of the children.

Tess Hurson:
That isn't what I was proposing, Patricia. In fact, I wasn't talking about custody at all, particularly. What I was trying to get at, by using a specific case, was the somewhat wider issue of how men do or do not these days, as opposed to twenty years ago, get involved in sharing responsibility.

Dominica McGowan:
Saying that men are more able to participate in caring for their children, is not the same as saying it's easier for women to encourage their men or their partners to look after their children. Those two things are separate from one another. I agree with you. My experience with many women is that, in situations where men want to participate more fully in child rearing and so on, not uncommonly women will exclude them. But I think that's because very often that's the only role women see for themselves, they think it's the only thing they're any good at, and they feel threatened. When someone tries to take that away from them and they're not getting something in exchange, they'll hold on to that.

Patricia Feeney:
But the basic thing is that a family has to live and they have to earn money; and in the world as it is, the person who can earn most money will, if there is a choice, be the one who works. Now, because of discrimination in employment, as well as unemployment, particularly discrimination in wage levels, in most cases it's not feasible that the man be the carer, because the woman can't earn enough money.

Mina Wardle:
I've gone through two generations of this. I've been married twenty-nine years. Both of us have worked through all our married life. We were equal wage-earners all our married life, but the responsibility for the children was mine – even though we were equal in every other way. And I don't know, but the children saw me as the person who responded the most to them. I don't know if it was just my personality or not. Now I see a bit better. I think it's probably

because I've been working with a lot of women, because now my husband's a grandfather and I'm a grandmother, and for the first time in twenty-nine years I've seen him change nappies, take babies out in prams, consider their education – all the things that were left to me. And I don't think it's because it's a grandchild.

Because of many television programmes, probably, he sees that men should have this role, and he's sticking his nose in. If he'd done that with his own children, we'd have been in heaven; but he didn't. Maybe it's because of women educating **him**. It's not considered menial to change a nappy, to worry about children's education, and so on. In twenty-nine years I've seen a difference in him. There's another thing about society: until about twenty years ago, grandparents were used as baby-sitters. I wouldn't have left my children with anybody only their grandparents, so therefore it has changed. When you say twenty years, child-minding centres are comparatively new. I know a lot of people would say: 'In twenty years, they should have done more'. But an awful lot of people have done an awful lot of work that's edging towards a better situation.

Edna Longley (The Queen's University of Belfast):
I agree with that. The very slow process of generational change is slower here than in other parts of the world. This is such a traditional society. There are plenty of examples of women internalizing patriarchal values, as feminists would say, whether it's the men coming to the day-care centre, or it's Maureen's encounter with Irish women talking about their strong sons, and getting status through their role. That's very strong, particularly in Irish nationalist culture: that's what you do, that's what the woman's role is.

There's one point that hasn't been mentioned, and that's the sectarian difference. On the general map of discrimination, on the one hand there's the whole area of discrimination against women through the state, in which women are equally disadvantaged in both communities; but the disadvantage is proportionately greater in the Catholic community. It's very important that, when women are on that general map, that should be minutely plotted. And then there is also the question as to whether there is a difference between experiences of women within the working class, in so far as they are segregated into Protestant and Catholic communities. Do different issues, different problems come up there? I actually do think it is as a result of the permeation of liberal, secular values from elsewhere, from America, from Europe, that a dent has actually been made in awareness in such a markedly traditional place.

I do think women have been prominent in addressing small issues – one step at a time. One example I heard the other day was the issue of strip-searching. According to Monica McWilliams of the University of Ulster, it was the women in the trade union movement – across the sectarian divide – who wanted to change that practice. It didn't involve the men from the beginning. They would not have got the changes that were eventually procured. Women can act as a kind of collective lobby on particular issues of discrimination that affect all women.

Even if you look at the Ulster middle class, you can see, on both sides, that it's markedly sexist. I'm now involved, to a certain extent, with Women's Studies in Queen's; and changing Queen's, changing courses in Queen's, changing structures in Queen's is proving a remarkably slow and painful business. We do have women coming into Queen's and the University of Ulster from working-class communities, mature women students – a wonderful phenomenon. The more we get of them, the more it helps us to change ourselves.

To give just one example: a woman we had last year, a mother of three sons, a Catholic woman. She could never cure herself of the habit of going home and making the tea for these three sons, all working. But she had one big triumph at the end of the year. There was a young priest at a novena, who was preaching about sin and what sins are. This was cast in a very patriarchal form. And the example he gave of patience, and how you could be a better person, was of a woman dealing with a drunken husband: 'you must try and be patient'. And he gave other examples of the responsibility of women bearing with men. But she went up to this priest afterwards (an unheard of thing for her to do, given her cultural circumstances) and objected: 'I found very offensive what you were saying in the pulpit'. She was very nervous and was trembling all over when she did it, and even when she told us about it, but I think she changed the awareness of that priest.

Tony McCusker (Central Community Relations Unit, Northern Ireland Office):
I'm not sure if I'm only supposed to be one of the listeners – I'm as much a part of this community as anybody else is, and the fact that

I'm a civil servant shouldn't make any difference! But anyway–Joan talked about bringing the debate into a wider constituency. This worried me slightly. This group represents about 8 or 9 per cent of the people here today. It's not getting a good audience. The plenary session will, I suspect, be dominated by the other issues.

In the area of government where I'm working, to do with equality issues – mainly on the religious front –we are trying to educate people about what the issues are. One of the things we found is that things that are maybe perceived by Catholics as being discriminatory are not actually perceived by Protestants in that way. In fact, they don't actually understand that that is how Catholics feel about certain things: for example, if you drive through the gates of Stormont and Carson is standing there with his finger out, that you would feel a chill factor going past that statue; or if you go into Stormont House, that the huge portrait of the Queen provides a chill factor for some Catholics.

I wonder, on women's issues as well, are there just as many things that men don't understand? I readily admit to being on a steep learning curve, because I come from a background where the traditional role of women –my mother and my sisters – was very, very traditional; and I expected that that was how life would go on for me. But in coming to grips with a lot of these issues, I've just this worry that if the debate takes place slightly to the side of where the main issues are being debated, it gets lost. That worried me today about this workshop. Would it be more powerful if these issues, these points, were forced into the mainline debate?

The second thing is something that came up some years back when they brought in the legislation on fair employment discrimination, and they debated whether you should have an all-embracing equality commission. I don't think the debate actually took place about that, in the sense of realistically thinking out the issues involved. I think, from discussions with people now, that there is this feeling of women's issues and discrimination against women being marginalized again and the issue of religious discrimination dominating everything.

The other point I just wanted to mention briefly was the education issue. Education worries the life out of me in so many ways, in terms of the values it leaves with children. You try to bring them up, in terms of roles and so forth, but within days it's gone, not only by contact with the other children, but by contact with the teachers. It's so obvious. And the paradox in that (in my circumstances – I'm not sure to what extent it's repeated elsewhere) is that predominantly, in primary school, the teacher is a woman.

Patricia Feeney:
You're right, of course; but that whole area of education is such an enormous one, with a whole variety of minute discriminations. But it involves the absorption, by very good citizens, of the patriarchal values of society. It's the people who have been the best pupils at school who become the teachers. Most teachers (despite the idea in England that they're all lefties – that's certainly not right) belong to a very conservative group in society. They have absorbed the mores of the society better than most, and they then pass them on; and because they are teachers they are passing them on better than most.

There's one big issue that was touched on very briefly, but in Ireland, north and south, it's very fundamental with regard to the position of women, and that is the influence of the churches. Even though the Catholic Church has very obvious discrimination, in terms of banning contraception, you will, nevertheless, find the attitudes in all of the churches more patriarchal than in any other sphere. And because the churches have such a big influence – even people who don't actually attend churches subscribe to them – they have a huge impact. It would be a brave Catholic woman would tell her mother that she wasn't going to church. There are expectations in the society. Even amongst Catholic women, whom I would know best, you'll only find within a very small group of friends that they'll admit to using contraception. You'll find a lot of people doing things in secret which are breaches of the Church's code, which they think that society will consider them less worthy if they admit to.

And it isn't just in the Catholic Church, because there are people who really don't subscribe at all to what the churches stand for, but if all their neighbours go to church, that is sufficient social pressure. If, for example, a little old lady (to use Una's phrase) is among her friends in church, then that's her social circle; and she goes to make the tea and arrange the flowers and organize the church functions and so on; and the men come along and they all flutter around. It happens – it doesn't matter which church. The Catholic Church is very obvious because of the contraception issue. But it permeates everything, because of the patriarchal normalization of our children.

Mina Wardle:

That certainly applies to the Protestant churches as well, because of their stance on divorce. I was actually denied the receiving of holy communion for fourteen years because I happened to have had a divorce. I was told I would not be allowed to be secretary of the Mothers' Union any more; and because of the fact that I was divorced and was actually considering remarriage, I definitely would not be able to receive holy communion. I actually drove fifty miles every Sunday and had communion in a church where nobody knew me, and that went on for fourteen years. So people feel like that in the Protestant churches as well.

Edna said she thought there was generally more discrimination in the Catholic community than the Protestant community. Well, I would disagree with that. I would think that the Protestant community just wasn't aware of the discrimination; but they are aware now. We were told we were God's own people, Stormont would look after us, and all the rest of it. We don't believe that any longer. We haven't believed that for thirty years, and we're fighting back. I don't feel discrimination is any less on the Protestant side than it is on the Catholic side. I think all women suffer the same discrimination, whether it be by the church or by the state or anywhere else.

[LUNCH BREAK]

Tess Hurson:

In this afternoon's session, we have to work towards the preparation of a report back to the plenary session, with a number of specific recommendations, if we wish.

Dominica McGowan:

Could the procedure used to gather evidence to make proposals about educational innovations such as EMU be used to generate recommendations for changing the curriculum in relation to gender discrimination?

John Watson (Pax Christi, Belfast):

Education for Mutual Understanding is something that has been going on over a number of years, a lot of it in isolation. Mr Mawhinney, who was Minister of Education, consulted a number of people, about how to carry it further. One suggestion made was that education for mutual understanding should spread generally throughout Northern Ireland, in all schools.

But I was reading a book recently, the results of an American study, which pointed out that books can be changed, the sex-stereotyping books can be thrown out, but the teachers still remain. It doesn't matter what sort of books you have, it's the teachers who direct kids towards courses, who direct them towards careers, and so on, so you have to change the teachers. And the only way you change teachers is: gather the information, get it into the training colleges, and eventually those teachers will go into schools. But you also need to have the Department of Education involve themselves in courses, where they will point out to teachers who haven't a clue, who don't know that they are promoting sex stereotyping. If you simply write it into the curriculum, teachers will say: 'My God, another thing we've got to teach. When will we get the time for it?' You integrate it subtly.

Dominica McGowan:
Well, except that the assumption is still there that the teachers will be on our side. That the teachers themselves are not stereotyping, and that they're divorced from the rest of the patriarchal world. The assumption is that teachers are these people who agree with what you're suggesting, John, and will then implement it.

Tess Hurson:
I think that what you're suggesting, John, is that this should be integrated into teacher training. By the time they're trained, there are so many pressures already on them. If you have to start somewhere, maybe the training college is the place to start.

Edna Longley:
It should be combined with education in universities, not just in training colleges. And that's a very slow and gradual process.

Tess Hurson:
Are there other proposals that people would like to make, specifically about education or training? One thing that I'm thinking about, as a sort of prompt to you, is the phenomenon in the last ten years or more of an enormous growth in adult and continuing education; and within that growth, a very heavy enrolment by women in adult and continuing education. By far, the biggest

percentage of people involved in adult education are women. There's great excitement among women about this. But they are also experiencing considerable problems to do with indirect inequality, in terms of crche facilities and so on, in terms of psychological difficulties with husbands or partners or fathers, who are not very keen on them being involved in adult education. Are there recommendations that we'd want to make about this large percentage of women in adult education?

Maureen Alden:
Could colleges of further education be asked to run career conferences and to concentrate, perhaps, on the needs of these women mature students? Because it wouldn't be the same for them as for an 18-year-old, since they've got more responsibilities.

Tess Hurson:
I think you're really making two points there, if I understand you correctly. One ties up with something that we were talking about earlier: the sort of interface between education and the workplace, or the implications of education in terms of the way women are disposed within the workplace. Designing courses to meet, in a more tailor-made way, the needs of the people who are actually enrolling for them is something that I think a lot of FE colleges (if only because of market forces) are having to consider. So I'm not sure that we need a recommendation. I think that the actual educators out there are fairly tuned in, and that people are beginning to look themselves and become confident enough to actually go to FE colleges and say: 'This is the sort of course we want'.

However, we may want some kind of recommendation that has to do with one of two things: with courses that have to do more specifically with things like self-development, which would tend to create more confidence among women. Again, there are quite a few of those being developed. Or, do we want a recommendation that concentrates on trying to alert educators, the people who are in charge, who have the funding, who are developing courses, to the necessity of courses that allow women paths into careers that traditionally they would not have moved into?

Maureen Alden:
And to encourage them to take courses that they tend not to take.

Tess Hurson:

Yes. The traditional pattern is that women tend to take arts courses, isn't that right? And the fellows take engineering and those sorts of courses. So, should we develop on from the implications of the first recommendation a second recommendation that links education to the workplace at the level of adult education, so that the recommendation would have something to do with trying to alert colleges (and FE colleges, particularly) to encouraging women to take courses in disciplines that are not traditional to them; and to make it a part of that that there are more careers conferences, with much more input from industry and the workplace.

Mina Wardle:

I think that what we should be doing here is creating a package to present as a recommendation to the Department of Education, or whoever we decide to present it to. We were talking about teacher training, we were talking about further education. Now, I think it would be unfair of me to leave that without saying that people that I work with would like an actual inquiry into primary school education. In the area I work in, the Shankill Road area, there were thirteen children who passed the 11-plus exam out of 373 who actually sat the 11-plus. Why has that happened? Why are children being told not to even bother to sit the 11-plus, which has actually happened in the school? 'Don't even bother – you're not capable'. We know that one group of children were told by a teacher: 'You're girls, what are you going to do with it if you do get it?' Now, I resent that, because it happened at my own school. It seems to me that there has to be an inquiry into this. Because nobody could tell me that there are no bright children in that area.

Dominica McGowan:

I don't think it's about brightness. I don't think that anybody would argue that the selection procedure is about brightness, when only 27% are allowed to pass anyway.

Mina Wardle:

They're talking now about adult education for women who were originally denied it. We don't want, in thirty years time, for these kids to have to go and learn basic educational skills, which is what women are having to do now. That is something that should be available to them now, and it's not.

Tess Hurson:
It's almost commonplace that opportunities generally are not as
good in working-class areas as they are in other areas.

Dympna McGlade:
I think we should focus on young female children. There has been
some research proving that teachers, whether consciously or unconsciously, discriminate in favour of boys, in the primary school
situation in particular. The Equal Opportunities Commission probably have overall statistical information on primary school children. This is the workshop for discrimination against women; and
I think we need to concentrate on female children.

Una O'Higgins O'Malley:
I do think language has an awfully important part to play. I'm
thinking, for instance, of all the recent references to finding a
'chairman' for these talks in Northern Ireland. That's a good
example of how at least half of the electorate is ruled out of the
running by simply not using the correct language for an important
position like that. On radio, for example, we hear stockbrokers
talking about clients, shareholders, and so on, and before long
they're saying how 'he' will be urged to reinvest in such and such.
So often still it all comes back to 'him', and the householder is
always 'he'. I do think we ought to mention that.

Tess Hurson:
Perhaps we could make a recommendation, particularly to the
media, to be more aware and sharper about the use of gender-
discriminating terminology.

Una O'Higgins O'Malley:
And to the churches.

John Watson:
May I make two very short points? One to this conference itself:
that men should feel that they should be able to attend this
workshop. There are mainly women here. I think that's disgraceful. If anything, men need to take part in this type of workshop
more and more, to learn, and to help break down the stereotypes
and not simply leave it to (what they would call) 'a group of
women'. The other point is: I would love to see branching out in a

full office situation Dorothy Eagleson's Educational Guidance
Service for Adults, which is now shut away somewhere in Bryson
House, part of another body. I would like to see somebody set up a
group which will do now for women what was done in the early
sixties to promote the whole idea of adult education. My wife
actually started with Dorothy, and ended up a barrister.

Dominica McGowan:
In 1978, Lord Melchett published a document which contained
policy objectives for his department. It was quite far-reaching. It
was very strongly recommended that, for some disadvantaged
groups and also for women, there was a need for child-care facilities. Now, I know there was a lot of sexism in there, but it was a very
good starting point, and these recommendations were supposed
to be put into operation. The minimum requirement of Melchett
in 1978 was that nursery provision here should be at least at the
level available in England. I know it's appalling in England, but it's
even more appalling here. In 1988 or '89, the Department conducted another investigation, and they found that none of those
recommendations had been implemented.

I would like to see a recommendation today, that the 1978
recommendations should be implemented immediately. Now, they
weren't comprehensive at all, but they were a very good starting
point. One of the main recommendations (which I thought was
excellent) was that there should be a consultative body, incorpo-
rating the Department of Education, the DHSS, the local Boards,
training units, schools, industry, the Planning Department, the
Housing Executive, community groups, voluntary groups, and
parents. This wide-ranging consultative body would determine
needs. But as a start, what we are entitled to is the level of provision
that there is in the rest of the UK. That would be a recommendation to the relevant minister.

John Fisher:
Could I suggest one more recommendation, to the Secretary of
State? A greater effort should be made to involve women in public
service. Only about 22% of persons serving on public bodies in
Northern Ireland are women.

Tess Hurson:
Another issue that came up this morning was the position of

carers. This is an issue that cuts across urban and rural areas, and probably also cuts across class divides. It's also symptomatic of the way in which women are perceived as being the ones who Automatically do the caring. Are there any particular recommendations that we could make, that would to some extent help to deal with or address that at all?

Mina Wardle:
Well, what I was talking about this morning, Tess, was that most of the carers that I know are either unmarried people or widowed people who had to give up their career to look after their parents. Once the parents die, these people find themselves stranded. I think there should be some sort of on-going financial assistance for these people, who have given up very good jobs, sometimes, to look after their parents – some kind of bridging assistance, for a couple of years, or until they find suitable employment again.

Tess Hurson:
Would it also be a good idea to recommend that further resources be made available for the counselling and retraining of women carers? Including people looking after disabled relatives; those carers nearly always turn out to be women as well. And in general, far more resources should be devoted to community care, given that this is now such a big emphasis after the Government White Paper. They need to be much more serious about backing that community care with financial resources for training people, and for a much wider and more integrated support network for community care.

I have also taken note of one final recommendation: that the Irish Association consider electing more women presidents! I do thank you all for your participation.

DISCRIMINATION IN EMPLOYMENT
AND UNEMPLOYMENT

Bob Cormack (The Queen's University of Belfast):
I thought it might be helpful to try to draw up an agenda of topics
that we should try to discuss. Maybe we should talk about discrimination first of all, and ask: 'What does it really mean?' And then we
could go on to talk about 'direct' and 'indirect' discrimination, as
those terms are used in the area. Then there is the question of
employment and unemployment differentials. Perhaps we don't
need to be too delayed on that – I think we're all fairly familiar
with what the differentials are. One of the things that has come
out over the time since the 1971 census is that we're seeing the rise
of a new Catholic middle class. I think it's worth talking about that
new Catholic middle class: who they are, what they're doing, what
we know about them. David McKittrick wrote a very interesting
article on this in *The Independent* a couple of months ago, and I
think it's worth spending some time on that.

I hear a lot of stories about Protestant perceptions and fears about
fair employment. I hope someone will want to voice some of these
perceptions. Tom Hadden focused on male unemployment. I think
that we should look at the differences between males and females,
Protestant and Catholic, and explore what the implications might
be. We might want to look at the fair employment legislation. What
do we think of it? Is it likely to be successful? What are the strengths
of it? Where are the weaknesses? Then there are perceptions of
fairness. Tony Gallagher might be able to say something, from the
recent social attitudes survey in Northern Ireland, about people's
perceptions of fairness; and under that topic we might talk about
the chill factor and people's perceptions of particular companies
and the difficulties that may be there in recruiting.

Employability – I'm thinking here about educational qualifications and training schemes; the appropriateness of training schemes;

the lack of availability of training, and so on. I'm very concerned that we often focus on Belfast, and really there may be considerable differences throughout the Province. It may be worth spending some time in teasing out any differences that we might know about.

The location of industry has always been a topic, particularly IDB, LEDU, government policies, and how this might affect the unemployment differential.

Apart from Government and government quangos, I thought we could also address community self-help projects and how they may help to address the problems.

Finally, one of the things that comes out of the Fair Employment Commission's monitoring returns is that in a small town you can find a company that's 90% Protestant and a company that's 90% Catholic; and employment (for the sake of argument) may be reasonably distributed between the two communities in that town. But one firm is nearly 100% Protestant and one is nearly 100% Catholic. Are we willing to accept 'separate but equal', if we got to the stage when there was equal employment but separate employment? Are we willing to accept that, or do we want to go further than that?

OK. Anyone like to kick the ball off on discrimination? Is the 'no blacks, no coloureds, no taigs need apply' direct discrimination of the past as virulent in the present, or is there now a veneer? Or have things changed, so that direct discrimination is no longer the real problem, and the real problem now is indirect forms of discrimination?

David McKittrick (British Irish Association; Ireland correspondent of _The Independent_):
In a historical sense, it seems to me that at the start of the troubles you had a situation where Britain hadn't been interested or particularly involved in the Northern Ireland situation. There was an amount of discrimination about before then; and the unionist community was faced with a dilemma when British interest and world interest awoke, because the principal Catholic allegation was that this is an unfair state and Catholics are being discriminated against.

The unionists had two choices at that point. Either they could say: 'No, there's no discrimination', and deny it completely. Or else they could say: 'Well, yes, there is discrimination, but it's justified. It's justified on our terms, because we're afraid of the

Catholic birth rate, we're afraid of Catholic voting patterns, we're afraid of housing and job patterns. We're afraid of all that changing, and there's a disloyal minority which doesn't deserve the same standards as unionist Protestants'. In general, the Protestants decided that they couldn't get into that second response, of admitting discrimination and trying to justify it. So they had to fall back on saying: 'No, there has been no discrimination'. That has been the general unionist response; and since then they have been trying to square that with the historical facts. That has been built into unionist politics since then, and it's a sense of guilt which they have never come to terms with.

Billy Hutchinson (Springvale Inter-Community Development Project, Belfast):
Could I just say something there? I'm Project Director of the Springvale Inter-Community Development Project on the Springfield Road, involving both Protestants and Catholics. Working-class Protestants were never guilty of discrimination. They were suppressed – not as much as the Catholics, but they were suppressed. People in Protestant areas worked for low wages; and the reason they did it was to keep Catholics out of jobs, because they were being told by the unionists that controlled them that they had to keep the Catholics out of power, and that was one way of doing it. I think this has to be cleared up: working-class Protestants were discriminated against. They weren't third-class citizens (the Catholics were third-class citizens), but working-class Protestants were second-class citizens, and they never colluded with the Unionists. They didn't have the power to collude. They acquiesced, but they never colluded.

Jamie Delargy (Journalist and Producer, Ulster Television):
I heard a recent programme on South Africa, talking about apartheid, and to my surprise it was clear from the interviewees that to approve of apartheid had become socially unacceptable. I think, in the same way, that has happened in Northern Ireland: to actively approve of discrimination, to say: 'Yes, it's absolutely right to give the jobs to our own people' (whatever side that might be – generally it's Protestants because Protestants enjoy greater power), that has become socially unacceptable. I don't think people in polite company would stand up and say: 'I do it and I'm quite proud of it; my company never employs a Catholic'. I'm not saying

that that means discrimination has ended. Clearly it hasn't. But I think that that is an important step that has been taken.

Bob Cormack:
Yes, but I wonder. I think that's true. I think people are a bit more cautious about what they would say in those kinds of conversations. But it seems to me, it's often a kind of veil or a veneer. They may say something like: 'We need to be sure who we're taking in, we need to know where they come from, which community. We don't want somebody leaving a package here on a Friday night when we close up the shop'. They just find another reason for doing exactly the same as they did in the past.

Jamie Delargy:
That's certainly possible. Still and all, it's still a significant step, I think, that the outright 'I'm not ashamed of it, I do it, I give the jobs to my own' attitude is gone. I agree with you that that's not getting to the root of the problem.

Bob Cormack:
What has often happened in the past is that employers positively discriminated in favour of their own, rather than necessarily discriminating against those of the other sort, so that through informal networks people have given employment to those of their own community. My favourite example of that is: if you go back to the 1911 census, you find big differences between Methodists, Presbyterians, and Church of Ireland, because they equally were discriminating in favour of their own within their own community. And since the church was the centre of much social activity and social networks, one would imagine they passed things on within Presbyterianism, Methodism, and the Church of Ireland.

Bob Cooper (Chairman of the Fair Employment Commission):
I'm just a bit puzzled that you should go back to 1911. The 1991 census would show exactly the same pattern – perhaps not as significant differences, but there are, nevertheless, significant differences between the life chances (unemployment rates, and so on) of the various Protestant denominations, with Methodists on top, Presbyterians second, and the Church of Ireland at the bottom. The Church of Ireland are closer to Catholics, but obviously quite a long way above Catholics.

Arthur Green (The Irish Association):

I used to be an under-secretary in the Northern Ireland Civil Service, and I was secretary, at the beginning of the troubles, to the Cameron and Scarman Inquiries. But I have become a strong, violent, right-winger and libertarian and an opponent of fair employment legislation. It seems to me that we could go on about the past for a long time. But I do think that, structurally speaking, a great deal goes back to the fact that Northern Ireland was a devolved structure of the kind that it was. And in that sense, I think it is very important not to blame people, or even communities. The structure inherently was a sectarian structure, and we can't help that.

Since 1972, it seems to me that the great bulk of that has disappeared. But certainly, for the record, I must say that at the beginning of the troubles I did genuinely write the bits of the Cameron Commission Report which dealt with discrimination, and I really accepted that position totally. But I now think that we went too far, and I actually have moved back towards the centre on this. I think if one reads Christopher Hewitt's book, for instance, there's a great revisionist piece of work that needs to be assimilated. I think we're too ready to stick with the interpretations that arose at the beginning of the troubles.

Oliver Kearney (Fair Employment Trust):

I'm representing two voluntary organizations, the Fair Employment Trust and the Equality Working Group. I'm an active campaigner in support of the McBride Principles and, unlike Arthur, very much in favour of very tough fair employment legislation. Could I pick up a couple of points? First, the very useful overview which David gave us. I think that the perception which he was offering to us would certainly be the sort of perception with which I would concur. It was my impression that about 1969 to '70, there was a sense of shock within the Protestant unionist community. The effect of the Cameron Commission Report, of the type of leadership being offered by Terence O'Neill, had created an environment in which many employers were for a period of time actually motivated towards trying to create better balanced workforces, without compulsion.

That attitude changed significantly in 1974. The UWC strike was a seminal experience for the Protestant community and rose out of a recognition of the fact that the Catholic invasion was actually

taking place. And from 1974 onwards, the process of discrimination then hardened once again, but became less open and una-
shamed (as Jamie described it), and became rather more sophisticated. There was a veneer laid across it. So not many employers
would readily concede today that they had discriminatory structures, or that they actively discriminated. What they would say, in
fact, is: 'We've never taken account of the religious make-up of our
work-force, and we really don't want to, and to impose it upon us is
a very sectarian thing to do'.

But, in fact, the process of word-of-mouth recruitment – of
father, son, relatives, and so on – is still very active and alive. A very
reputable Protestant clergyman with whom I had a frank conversa-
tion a short time ago said to me: 'You need to understand that
fathers wish to protect what their fathers built up and to pass it on
to their children'. So it would seem to me that, while the management of discrimination in employment has changed and has become somewhat more sophisticated and rather more respectable,
the processes are still very active. Down at the level at which you
were talking about, Billy, I understand very deeply your comment,
that the Protestant working class never had power. They didn't. All
the Protestant working class could ever aspire to was favours being
passed down. But the favours are still being passed down.

Billy Hutchinson:
I'd like to know what they are! I live in a two-up two-down, just the
same as people living in the Falls. I suffered from the same depri-
vation that they did. If you compare the education system in
Protestant West Belfast and Catholic West Belfast, Catholic West
Belfast is streets ahead of us, their education system is far superior.

Arthur Green:
I take it Oliver isn't suggesting that it's one-sided. I think he's
talking about both communities doing this discriminatory thing.
Bob, you were quoted, a few weeks ago, as saying that the survey
that has been done of the top 200 firms showed this very substantially on both sides. I don't think we should be tremendously
disturbed about this.

Bob Cooper:
Broadly speaking, what comes out from the monitoring information is the very great degree of segregation there is in employment.

One of the things which people keep saying about Northern Ireland is that it's great that we've kept sectarianism out of the workplace, and that people fight each other at night and then come in and work happily with each other the next day. To which I sometimes reply, perhaps slightly cynically: 'Would that that were true'. The reality is that they don't actually work together during the day. What the monitoring returns show, quite simply, is that there is an enormous degree of segregation in employment. I think it is possibly an economic rule, that in a situation of segregation, the weaker community is likely to be the sufferer. And that is indeed the case.

I have a chart which shows the private-sector monitored firms and the extent to which they accord with the religious composition of the travel-to-work area. The curve is what you would expect, if there was no segregation. But the chart shows how few of the firms are inside the curve. These are single-site firms, about 1,360 of them. Of those 1,360 firms, Catholics were grossly under-represented in almost 500. In 250, Protestants are grossly under-represented. Substantially more than half the firms are firms where there is gross under-representation of one community or the other. Segregation is something which we, as the Commission, have to tackle very strongly.

There is a respectable argument which says that we should not be concerned with a company where Catholics are over-represented, where there are too few Protestants, since the overall object of the exercise, of the legislation, is to equalize the life chances of both communities. I think the argument against that is quite simply that segregation in itself is something that we have to be concerned with, for all sorts of social reasons; but also because in all circumstances in which you have that kind of situation, it is the weaker community that suffers.

Arthur Green:
Would you not agree with the point that Graham Gudgin and his colleague make, which does seem to me to suggest that the actual balance is now surprisingly similar, as between the communities.

Bob Cooper:
I think there's a great deal of misunderstanding of what the discrepancy of $2^1/2$ times Catholic unemployment means for the people who are in employment. An awful lot of people thought

that what that meant was that the proportion of people in employment who are Catholic is very low. But statistically, if you start working it out, what you find is that if Catholics are 37% of the total economically active labour force, and they are 36% of those in employment, their unemployment rate is 30% higher than Protestants. If they are 35% of those in employment as opposed to 37% in the labour force, they have a 60% greater unemployment rate than Protestants. And if they are 3% less, 34% as opposed to 37%, they have an unemployment discrepancy of somewhat over 2 to 1, broadly speaking. So that a 3% under-representation of Catholics is sufficient to create an unemployment discrepancy of more than 2 to 1. Therefore, as I say, when people look at the figures and say: 'This is surprising, 34% of people in employment are Catholic', they don't recognize that you're working a fine margin – and the big difference that can make in unemployment.

Arthur Green:
Quite. But Gudgin's particular point really was the way in which the social profile of those in employment seemed to be levelling out.

Bob Cooper:
I think that it is levelling out, to an extent. I would just make one very important caveat about those figures, which show that Catholics are actually ahead of Protestants in the managerial, professional, and technical groups of occupations. That is so, if you take the three top occupation groups all together: first of all, managerial; secondly, professional; and thirdly, technical and associated professional. But Catholics are ahead overall for one very simple reason. They're under-represented in the first one, they're under-represented in the second one, but they're significantly over-represented in the third one. So when you take all three together, you'll find that Catholics have a slightly higher proportion than Protestants.

The reason they're over-represented in the third one is that that is the occupation in which nurses figure. There are an awful lot of nurses in Northern Ireland, and they are significantly over-represented with Catholics. So in essence, when you are saying that Catholics have a higher proportion of those three groups taken together, you're saying it's because Catholics have a much higher proportion of nurses. In British terms, this is an occupation that used to be filled by Irish people and by West Indians. In other words, it is normally an occupation which wasn't in very great demand. So I think it is somewhat dangerous to put too much emphasis on that, because of the over-representation of Catholics among nurses.

Arthur Green:
How do you assess the work of Paul Compton on this question of the relative unemployment rates?

Bob Cooper:
One thing that Paul Compton totally ignores is that all of the factors which he takes into account as explaining the discrepancy in unemployment are factors which are in themselves shaped by discrimination in the past. It's a circular argument to say that Catholics have a higher rate of unemployment because they are in lower social classes. They are in lower social classes largely because they were discriminated against as Catholics in the past.

Arthur Green:
The point of Paul Compton's position is to suggest that the differential in unemployment can be explained by structural factors. That is a respectable position, and it's very important, because we end up in a position where the issues that provoked all of us twenty years ago have, in fact, changed their context.

Bob Cormack:
We had a session with Paul Compton two days ago, and it seemed to me we were rehearsing the past. These arguments had been made in the early '80s; and what Paul doesn't do is address his critics. He continues to produce the arguments in the way that he did in a paper in 1981.

But let's think where we're going. We're still on discrimination. We've also talked about the results of the FEC monitoring return and the highly segregated nature of many work-forces. To finish with the discrimination part. What does seem to be happening is that you've still got an awful lot of informal networks operating to recruit people into employment, and that's reproducing existing patterns. How much of the old-fashioned direct discrimination is still going on we don't really know. I think the point to make here is that it's about time we had some of those discrimination tests done in Northern Ireland. Tony Gallagher, would you like to explain how that might be done?

Tony Gallagher (Centre for the Study of Conflict, University of Ulster):
These types of tests have been carried out on a number of occasions in Britain, looking at the depth of discrimination against ethnic minorities. The standard procedure is to make a lot of bogus applications for jobs, coming from people who are from one group or another, and look at the outcomes of those applications. It's a relatively straightforward exercise. There was one point where it was nearly done, as part of the investigation by the Standing Advisory Commission on Human Rights [SACHR], but for a variety of reasons it wasn't carried out. There has never, as far as I'm aware, been any academic study that has directly tried to examine the extent to which direct discrimination continues to exist in Northern Ireland.

If I could take up one point from what Oliver was saying about the informal networks. There is a lot of evidence that those informal networks, or indirect discrimination, continue to play an important role. That SACHR investigation found that an awful lot of employers quite freely admitted that they used various informal networks to recruit people. But that still doesn't address Bob's question of the extent to which direct intentional discrimination, of a relatively crude type, continues to exist. Picking up again from something that Oliver was saying, if it was the case that there still is a lot of that intentional discrimination, then it's perhaps a little odd that so many employers appear to be quite happy to engage in the monitoring exercise. There was a lot of talk before the first monitoring exercise, that perhaps there would be all sorts of problems getting figures out of large numbers of companies. In practice, that didn't happen at all. But that's just a straw in the wind; and we still need a more direct examination of the issue.

Bob Cooper:
I am extremely keen to see such an exercise done. There's a big gap in our knowledge. We all have our own views, based on all sorts of things, about the extent to which direct, deliberate, intentional, line discrimination occurs. But there's not been any academic work on that, and we're extremely keen to see academic work on it. I should just express one word of caution.

According to David Smith of the Policy Studies Institute, when they were starting doing the work for SACHR, this was one of the areas which they had looked at doing, because they were the people who had done most of the work in Britain with regard to blacks. One of the things which forced him to back off at that particular time was that it is quite easy to do it in London, for example, where you have a labour market which is fairly tight, where there's not a vast bulk of people unemployed (or there wasn't at that time), and therefore you didn't have to do that many tests to get statistically significant figures. But his concern was that in the Northern Ireland situation, where perhaps you have a hundred applicants for every one job, there's a fairly strong chance that both your Protestant and Catholic testers are going to be turned down; and therefore you would have to do an enormous amount of testing to get statistically significant information. That may well be right.

Bob Cormack:
Anybody want to comment, from experience on the ground, on your impressions or perceptions of the degree to which this direct, crude discrimination is still continuing?

Oliver Kearney:
I didn't want to give the impression, in the comments I was making earlier, that direct, crude discrimination has disappeared. It hasn't.

Bob Cooper:
No, I don't think I would argue that it has disappeared. There is an argument about how much it happens. I suspect myself that direct discrimination is more common not in a situation where you have the Protestant candidate who is grossly underqualified and the Catholic candidate who is very well qualified, but where you have Protestant and Catholic candidates who are much of a muchness, or maybe the Catholic candidate is a bit better than the Protestant candidate, and Protestant employers select the person who is of their own religion. I think that's where it's more likely to happen at the present time, rather than where there is a wide margin between the candidates. But that's an impression. I may be wrong in that.

Jamie Delargy:

I actually considered this for a programme, this idea of sending in bogus applications. But I think it's phenomenally difficult, because you need the co-operation of at least two schools. I think the Catholic school might be more easily persuaded to do it. But you also need the agreement of at least one Protestant school, because obviously, you have to identify very clearly that this particular person is a Catholic or a Protestant in the application form, and you need the agreement of a Protestant school to do that. I can't see it happening in Northern Ireland on a large scale. There would be so many people involved in the whole charade, that I concluded it had to be done by somebody with greater resources than a TV programme.

Arthur Green:

I believe the very basis of the fair employment legislation should be questioned. It does seem to me now a genuine question, and I don't think it can be dismissed as sectarian, because, if the statistics are not absolutely clear-cut (and I think they are not), the idea of segregating people by community is inherently extremely undesirable, by assuming that the difference of community is of such enormous significance. It's only of significance if the statistics are absolutely clear-cut. Take gender questions – you can't do anything about changing your gender. Take race questions – you can't do anything about changing your race. But in social relations in Northern Ireland, the question of which religion, which politics, is increasingly something which is subject to change, and we all know people who are cross-community, in those terms. So actually as an issue, I think the continued validity of the whole world of 'fair employment' needs to be questioned.

Bob Cormack:

Right. You're suggesting we move on to the differential and perhaps just look at the statistics. Where do we start? There's two-and-a-half times the male rate of unemployment for Catholics. I think it then becomes incumbent on you, if you're faced with that kind of problem, to specify what solution you are going to suggest.

Arthur Green:

The issue is whether the difference is a question of culpability, or whether it's something that in fact society ought to adjust. I have no doubt that there may be things to be said in detail about the Compton-type position, but his essential argument seems to me to be incontrovertible. That is, if you are dealing with structural differences between the communities, and you add all those up, you end up with the position where the differences explain themselves. My point is that one should not do this lightly. We all did this x years ago, of course. But the question is, is it justified? Because, with another part of our minds, we know that it raises tension between the groups which ought, in fact, to be melding and collaborating and being, in a certain way, indifferent to the differences between them.

Tony Gallagher:
There's a number of points can be made about that. I think it's important to set Paul Compton's work in a slightly wider context. The point has already been made, that when Paul Compton talks about the number of structural features explaining the unemployment gap, once you take those structural features into account, the unemployment differential disappears. Arguably, one conclusion you should derive from that is that those structural features which he has identified in themselves set an agenda for change. They set an agenda of the sort of features that need to be changed: such as location of jobs, so that you try to direct more jobs into West Belfast, say, where unemployment is very high; and you try to improve the training facilities in places like West Belfast. That's one point.

A second point with respect to the need for a wider context: there's another detailed statistical analysis that was carried out by David Smith of the Policy Studies Institute, where he also, using data from the Continuous Household Survey, looked at the unemployment differential and at a number of different structural elements, to try to see if they explained the unemployment differential. His analysis came to exactly the opposite conclusion from the one Paul Compton came to: that is to say, once you took those structural features into account, there still remained a very large element of the unemployment differential which wasn't explained.

His argument, in that particular study, was that this large bit of the unemployment differential that wasn't explained by these structural features was likely to be explained by direct or indirect discrimination. So, in the academic literature, you have these two positions that are exactly the opposite to each other. At the moment, there is some work being done to re-run those analyses, trying to get some sort of common picture. But I don't think that simply on the basis of one study the whole unemployment problem has changed.

Arthur Green:
No, I wouldn't like to lay too much stress on Compton alone. But it is obvious that at a minimum there is very, very great disagreement here. It is also true that a lot of people have criticized Smith's work, and so on; and it appears that the consensus has moved much more towards the centre on this than was the case previously.

Matt Wallace (Director of Worknet, Belfast):
I'm a bit disappointed with the discussion so far, and the whole emphasis on statistics. We all know there's discrimination, we all know there's injustice in places like West Belfast and North Belfast. But we're going over and over the same old ground. We who live in West Belfast have had scheme after scheme after scheme: YTS, ACE, YTP – we know every scheme inside out. Twenty pound a week, thirty pound a week, ten pound a week, we're no further on. As for all this analysing, we've heard it all, we've seen it all, we know it, we want to go forward.

Arthur Green:
I think that is fundamentally mistaken, because the issue is not whether there should or should not be high unemployment in a particular place; the issue is whether these differentials of employment can be used to justify the whole apparatus of the state. On the question of high unemployment in a particular area, you can obviously take different views, and you can take them outside Northern Ireland just as much. It's not unique to Northern Ireland.

Billy Hutchinson:
The problem in Northern Ireland is that the working-class people – it doesn't matter whether they're Protestant or Catholic – are disenfranchized. They can't remove the Tory Government which has caused high unemployment.

Matt Wallace:
I'm not sure that the senior civil servants, at decision-making level in Stormont, yet know the poverty and the social deprivation that

exist on the Falls and the Shankill. They've no empathy with the place, they've no understanding of the place. A senior civil servant recently admitted it was his first time in West Belfast, Falls Road or Shankill, in twenty years. He's a man who's supposed to be making decisions for us and on behalf of us. I would agree with Billy one hundred percent: Falls or Shankill aren't a bit different. We work together as best we can, in fact. It's the same in the Shankill, there's scheme after scheme after scheme. We're implementing all the things that Government have asked us to do, but I'm not so sure that we're getting the return that is due to us.

Billy Hutchinson:
I'm a working-class Protestant. I had nothing to do with fifty years of misrule. People are talking about discrimination. According to a recent report published by the Belfast Centre for the Unemployed, the Shankill is third on the overall list of social deprivation in the Belfast City Council area. Court ward, in the Lower Shankill, is first on the poverty list. A 1989 survey carried out for the Greater Shankill Development Agency by Touche Ross showed that 78.3% of the people in Protestant West Belfast claim benefits, while 78.8% claim benefits in Catholic West Belfast. The people in Catholic West Belfast don't have jobs, but the people in Protestant West Belfast that do have jobs are low paid and they still have to claim benefit. It doesn't matter whether it's 50% poverty or 5% poverty, it's an indictment against the Government and it has to be eradicated. And getting rid of unemployment is one of the ways of doing that.

Bob Cormack:
Let's continue on with that. Let's hear what's going on, in terms of training schemes, and in terms of trying to bring industry into the area. What's happening with Montupet?

Billy Hutchinson:
Recently we were involved in a comprehensive economic development scheme. We set up a group to speak to people who were involved in economic regeneration. We went to see LEDU [the Local Employment Development Unit] and the IDB [the Industrial Development Board]. The IDB told us they could not separate an area out, such as Protestant West Belfast or Carrick. But after we went away after talking to them, we found out that they

had done just that. They took Antrim and they took Carrickfergus and said they had high levels of unemployment, and they were trying to encourage new investors into those areas.

Irrespective of the violence in West Belfast, most of the people don't control the violence, they've nothing to do with it. We can't tell the UVF or the IRA what to do or what not to do. We have to live there, and we have to work there. We want to keep up a campaign against this idea that it's terrorism that stops the creation of jobs. Father Matt has a lot of successful schemes; there are a lot of successful schemes on the Protestant side. There's a lot of cross-cultural stuff going on. It's been successful, up to a point. But we don't need any more schemes, it's jobs we need.

Matt Wallace:
I do believe we've reached saturation point now with schemes. They're a dead end. You asked about Montupet. Montupet said they didn't want skilled workers, that they would implement their own training programmes. I don't see much evidence of that at the moment. They offer some kind of training, with no guarantee of a job at the end. I'm not so sure that those undergoing the training will actually get jobs. The same thing happened with Debenham's, remember: a lot of these people came over from England. Short's are the same. Both of these are holding exercises.

Bob Cormack:
Tell us what happened with the Debenham's scheme.

Julie Cullen (Forum for Community Work Education):
Debenham's promised a lot of employment to people living in West Belfast and took a lot of people on in training schemes. I know one man who hadn't worked in years. He was told by Debenham's that he needed a suit. So he rigged himself out to go on this training scheme, as a trainee manager, and his target was a job at the end. They were all trained, but a very, very small percentage of them were actually employed. They were trained and dropped, and left deeper in debt. The whole thing just raised people's expectations.

Bob Cormack:
What about Montupet? You feel they haven't put on the training programmes that they suggested they would?

Matt Wallace:
As I understand it, they have a certain number of young men and
women training at the Boucher Road Training Centre at the
moment. I wouldn't like to say how many will actually get a job at
the end of the day. It's not as I was led to believe initially, that they
would bring them on site and train them. We made the point that
West Belfast is full of unskilled people; and they said that wasn't a
concern, that they would do the training themselves. I'm not in a
position to say what exactly is the structure of the work-force there
at the moment. Certainly, it's not affecting unemployment in West
Belfast as we thought it would.

Oliver Kearney:
Could I give you my interpretation of what's happening with
Montupet? Ford spent about £50 millions within the last decade in
restructuring their operation at Finaghy Road North in Belfast,
and in the process they shed 700 jobs; which, by the way, they use
as an explanation of the reduction in the Catholic proportion of
the work-force, because Ford claim that a very high proportion of
Catholics at that time accepted redundancy.

  Ford then entered into a joint agreement with Montupet that
Montupet would establish their operation (which is a components
manufacturing unit for Ford Britain) at Dunmurry; and Montupet
are now a main supplier to Ford Britain of a select component. As
are Ryobi, the Japanese firm at Carrickfergus, also a component
supplier. So, if at any time Ford Britain decides it no longer
requires the supply of those components, all it has to do is switch
off the tap, and Montupet then sheds its jobs, without in any way
impacting upon Ford. Likewise with Ryobi. Both Ryobi and
Montupet are recruiting their skilled craftsmen, supervisors, and
foremen from Short's and from Harland & Wolff; and they are
providing semi-skilled training opportunities, through the Boucher
Training Centre, to potential young employees from West Belfast.

Jamie Delargy:
Who encourages people to go on these schemes? Is it the Government, or is it the companies themselves?

Oliver Kearney:
A kid who's coming out of school either goes on a Job Training
Programme – which gives them the equivalent of the dole payment

plus, I think, £10 – or if they don't go on that, they don't get anything. So, technically they are no longer an unemployed person, they're a trainee for a period of six or twelve months, after which they then become unemployed.

Jamie Delargy:
But who encourages them specifically to go for these particular companies? There's an allegation that there's a wilful fraud, almost, that people are being invited to go for positions that don't exist. Is it the companies, or is it the Government?

Julie Cullen:
Under these new regulations, you have to be seen to be actively seeking employment. You're given two or three chances, and then your dole is cut. You've no choice. You can't go and say: 'I'd like to do this, or I'd like to do that'. You've no choice. And if there's a training scheme, you either accept it or lose your dole money.

Jamie Delargy:
So, if there's a case of a thousand people going forward, and there are actually only a hundred jobs or fifty jobs, are people telling them . . .?

Matt Wallace:
There might be only one job or no job. If there's only one job, they have to go. They have to fill in their forms; and unless they prove that they're active in the job market, actively looking for work, and have evidence of it, they get nothing.

Oliver Kearney:
We're maybe straying a little bit from your agenda here, Bob. The question is 'the differentials'. The unemployment differentials do exist. Whether they are structural, historical manifestations, or whether they are a combination of structural imbalance in the management of the economy (which I very strongly believe them to be, in relation to location of industry and the opportunity for economic development), combined with discrimination, is not really material to what I want to say now. The differentials do exist. We do know, from the demographic surveys, that there is a very high proportion of the young people aged fifteen years and downwards in Catholic schools who will be seeking employment, along

with young Protestants, over the next decade, but the proportion of young Catholics seeking employment will be higher. One can argue about whether it's 2% or 5% – the proportion will be higher than the proportion of young Protestants seeking employment.

Now, if unemployment differentials already exist, for whatever reason, and those needs are going to increase dramatically – as they will do over the next decade – and they cannot be met, then I think we are faced with a community crisis. We must either accept that there will be massive emigration outflow of young illegals to Australia, the United States, or the streets of London; or else we're going to increase enormously the proportion of young unemployed male and female Catholics, living under Father Matt Wallace's schemes, where he's trying to fill up the pot continuously. The proportion of unemployed is growing in Belfast, in Derry, in Cookstown, and in Dungannon; and it doesn't require a social scientist to recognize that the potential for the enlargement and the intensification of our community conflict is already upon us, and we ought to be looking for solutions for it.

Arthur Green:
I can see I'm casting myself in a sort of ghoulish role; but actually, I think that we have far too low migration rates. We have only half the rate of the Republic – the Republic's rate is twice as high as ours. And I think that we have got into the habit of staying put, in a way which is damaging. I quite agree with you, that the actual pressure on the jobs that are actually available is very substantial, but the answer unquestionably is higher migration. Apart from some palliative schemes.

Oliver Kearney:
That certainly worked for many generations, but unfortunately, people like the Americans and the Canadians and the Australians are not being so co-operative these days. It's going to be a lot more difficult.

Arthur Green:
You would agree, though, that it is a curious fact, that our rate is so much lower than the Republic's.

Matt Wallace:
I think that's a diversionary tactic again. In justice, our young people are entitled to work in their own country.

Arthur Green:
I don't thing so. I think that people should solve their own problems as much as possible. If that involves moving, they should
move. We should move.

Matt Wallace:
That's a terrible slur on the people of Ulster, it really is. You're
saying: 'Privatize the community'. Let people try to work out their
own future, without any support from anyone. That's a terrible
scenario, and a terrible reflection on Government.

Arthur Green:
The Government is already spending on an enormous scale, on a
disproportionate scale, in Northern Ireland. The question is
whether Government should provide a whole community with
income support on a substantial scale. There are limits. I actually
think that there is no question – we have far too many people
unwilling to move. Let me make it quite clear that I am speaking as
an individual. The Government's position is quite different. The
Government's position is to tinker and assist and do the best it can,
within certain constraints.

Bob Cormack:
A simple point on migration. The people who are migrating now
are the ones with qualifications and skills; but those who are
unqualified don't have the choice or the opportunity of emigrating.

Arthur Green:
Would you question my point, that our overall rate of migration is
far lower than in the rest of the island?

Bob Cormack:
What's happening in the South of Ireland is that they're exporting
their graduates.

Arthur Green:
Statistically, that can only be a small factor.

Bob Cormack:
You've surely got to build that in when you're looking at the
migration rates. Who are these people that are leaving? What skills

are they going with? What jobs are they going to at the other end?
The unemployed leaving Ireland and going to London to sleep in
cardboard boxes is no solution.

Matt Wallace:
Arthur, when you were under-secretary, did you ever visit West
Belfast, the Falls or the Shankill?

Arthur Green:
Certainly. My first visit to the Shankill and Falls was about 1955.
But don't tar Government with my indiscretions. Government
takes a much more centralist position than I do. But in a discussion like this, where we really are trying to deal with the basics of
the issues, I think one should raise the debate: how much is it
reasonable to expect from Government?

Bob Cooper:
Southern emigration is higher, but the crucial thing is that a lot of
the people who are leaving the South are not permanent emi-
grants; they go abroad for a while and then they come back. Now,
obviously a lot of people in the South aren't satisfied with that. But
it is different from the type of emigration which you would need if
you wanted to solve the unemployment problems of West Belfast. I
don't say that all emigration is, by definition, bad; but I would
accept, by definition, that it is not an answer to our problems of
unemployment.

Bob Cormack:
About a year ago, a reporter for *The Independent* interviewed some
Irish people in a London pub, and made the point that the old
acronym used to be WIMPEY – We Import More Paddies Every
Year. But the new one is NIPPLE – New Irish Professional People
Living in England. That's the difference.

Oliver Kearney:
I'd like very much if we could come on to the legislation. The
Government has provided £960 million to Short's to prepare it for
take-over by Bombardier, and £300 million over the last few years
to write off the debts in Harland & Wolff, to have it taken over by
Fred Olsen. I mentioned earlier the £50 million for Fords to strip
down 700 jobs. There were £20 million to Mackie's, in order to

rationalize it and have it taken over by Lummus Industries and move from the Springfield Road up into Woodvale. Against that, offset the £60 million which Richard Needham says he has been pumping in in the last twelve months, in a variety of ways, into West Belfast. Let's look at those sums in the context of the legislation that Bob Cooper's struggling with, and how that affects the whole question of not simply anti-discrimination fair employment legislation, but also legislation actively directed towards preventing discriminatory policies being evolved and pursued by the people who make the decisions in our society.

Linda Moore (Centre for Research on Women, University of Ulster):
I think it's really important to talk about Protestant perceptions and fears. As Tom Hadden reported them in his presentation, if you implement the fair employment legislation, working-class Protestants fear that they are automatically going to lose jobs.

Joe McWilliams (The Irish Association):
But why focus on Protestant perceptions and not Protestant **and** Catholic perceptions? I would have thought that fundamental to the problem here, apart from the analytical side, is the irrational side. Our problem has a large element of irrationality in it – some people say it's a psychiatric problem. And because of that, I think that perceptions are extremely important. People don't read statistics. They watch television, and they read newspapers, and they talk in pubs. It's at that level that the irrational is transmitted from one generation to the next.

I was formerly employed by The University of Ulster, and before I left, to run an art gallery, I was the only Catholic teaching on the course. I'm not complaining, although there was an imbalance. But what I'm talking about is the perception of some of the students. Because I was talking to one of them a year after she left, and she said: 'Of course, the Poly's coming down with Roman Catholics'. There's an awful implication in that comment: the implication is that one Catholic's too many!

Billy Hutchinson:
Recently I was asked to write an article for Community Relations, from the Protestant point of view. I actually agree with some of the things they're doing, but a lot of working-class Protestants don't

understand it and don't agree with what they're doing. When I spoke to some Protestant working-class friends about the Community Relations Council and about fair employment, they all lumped the two of them together and said they were only for Catholics and for tackling international opinion about what Northern Ireland's about, and for showing Americans that there was no longer any discrimination. I don't agree with that, but that's certainly what a lot of working-class Protestants feel.

Bob Cormack:
There is a lot of truth in that, inasmuch as the McBride campaign did keep the pressure on the Government through the period of developing the fair employment legislation.

Tony Gallagher:
On a similar theme, I was at a conference organized recently by the Transport and General Workers Union, on equality. One of the workshops had shop stewards talking about views from their workplaces on fair employment legislation, and those sorts of ideas were coming through very strongly. For an awful lot of people in the workplaces, as far as they're concerned, the fair employment legislation is about getting jobs for Catholics.

Joe McWilliams:
How do you counteract perceptions like that? If you're presenting statistics that say 75% are from one group, and 25% from the other, how do you convince someone who doesn't want to believe that? We have to educate that group of people in some way, and just producing statistics doesn't seem to be enough.

Billy Hutchinson:
I think the whole problem is that people always talk in terms of discrimination. My own opinion is that there just isn't enough jobs. We should be talking about getting people in there to create jobs. When we get the jobs in, I agree, the Catholics should get the jobs as well as Protestants, but I don't think they should be giving jobs to Catholics because they're Catholics or to Protestants because they're Protestants.

I live in Protestant West Belfast and I work on the edge of Catholic West Belfast. I see it day in and day out: the poverty, the social deprivation, the whole lot's there. If people got jobs, a lot of the sectarianism would disappear as well. These people have been told for years that the jobs aren't there. On the Catholic side it is bad, because they never had jobs. On the Protestant side, the people have had jobs for years. They now find themselves unemployed, or they find it harder to get work. And that whole process is getting worse. What I actually see is the Protestant areas taking on some of the problems they have in Catholic West Belfast. There's a lot of problems that they have, but we haven't got yet, but we'll get them soon, because the unemployment is rising.

Bob Cormack:
Back in the 1970s, my feeling about the problem of employment and unemployment in Northern Ireland was that it had to be changed by structural mechanisms; that you needed to tackle it through the Fair Employment Agency and the legislation. There was a sense also, in the 60s and 70s, that if you change people's attitudes, things could change. The Peace People were an example of that. I always took the opposite view: you change the structures first, and hopefully you change the attitudes as a result of having changed the structures, by forcing companies to hire from both sides of the community. It seems to me now that I'm beginning to change my mind again: that once you've got the structures in place, you're still left with the kind of problem that Bob Cooper was pointing out earlier. You can have a town where you've got very divided employment. There may even, hypothetically, be equal employment for both communities, but in separate firms; and then you're on to an attitudes/perception problem that has to be addressed as such.

Bob Cooper:
Could I make a couple of points about West Belfast? I think most people recognize nowadays that Protestant West Belfast is almost unique among Protestant areas. There is no question about it. It is substantially worse off than most other Protestant working-class areas, in terms of unemployment, in terms of opportunities. A number of things have contributed to this. One of them was the fact that Mackie's at one time employed 5,500 and now employs 700. They formerly recruited that number yearly. A high proportion of those were Protestants from West Belfast. The shipyard has gone from about 10,000 in the 1970s to less than 2,500. A significant number of those would have been from Protestant West

Belfast. So, Protestant West Belfast has lost out extremely badly, in that respect.

We have been talking about perceptions. Sometimes, of course, there's a grain of truth in perceptions; and when you say there is a perception that the Fair Employment Commission wants to get more Catholics jobs, that is not an entirely untruthful perception. The legislation would not have been enacted if it wasn't for the fact that there are too few Catholics in jobs. I would make one important point, however. One of the ways of getting the situation right is by making sure that all privileges which formerly attached to those who had jobs, who had family connections with jobs, who were the 'inner circle', as it were, have to be removed. And what that means is: the word-of-mouth recruitment, the jobs for friends and relations, and so on. The reason for removing that may be so that Catholics in West Belfast may have a better opportunity to get jobs. But it also means that Protestants in West Belfast will have better opportunities to get jobs as well. Because they have suffered also from the fact that they are not part of the inner circle.

So a policy that was designed specifically because of the problems of Catholics in West Belfast can actually have plus points for Protestant West Belfast as well. It's not a zero-sum situation exactly. It is most important that the removal of discriminatory practices means the removal of all those practices which discriminate against have-nots, whether they're Protestant or Catholic.

[LUNCH BREAK]

Oliver Kearney:
A gentleman from the Northern Ireland Office spoke to me in the lunch queue and said that, while Professor Hadden tended to go on a bit about security issues and didn't really understand the NIO's security policies, he was very pleased that at any rate he had given them a clean bill of health on fair employment – which I found a rather astonishing interpretation of what Professor Hadden had to say. But that's the NIO's interpretation!

I think, in a shrinking economy (and Bob Cooper, I know, would concur with this), that the imperatives to maintain discriminatory structures are even more powerful than they are in an expanding economy; and we have had the peculiar situation over the last decade or so, in which, concurrent with a shrinking economy in many areas such as manufacturing, we have also had an expanding economy in many areas such as financial institutions. Now, the inequality of Catholics in the manufacturing areas has actually worsened as a result of the shrinkage which has taken place. But Catholic equality has not advanced in those areas in which the economy has expanded. And one then has to examine what are the reasons for that, and what role fair employment legislation has to play.

I think the problem with fair employment legislation is that there is a fundamental contradiction in it. If we are living in a state which was established explicitly for the purpose of securing a Protestant economic domination, then discrimination – whether it's vicious and open, or structured and neat and clean – is the correct way to maintain the existence of the state. And if you introduce powerful fair employment legislation, which overturns that basis of domination and power, then by extension you are actually attacking the foundations of the state. We've been wrestling with this contradiction of effective fair employment legislation for a very long time; and I think working-class Protestants are right to feel threatened by fair employment legislation, because by implication it is going to give something more to Catholics than the economic structures of the state have been designed to give them. The only way in which, on the face of it, it can do that is by taking it away from working-class Protestants.

However, I'll have to be very provocative and say the legislation has failed. The legislation was designed for failure – and Bob Cooper knows my views on this, and it's no reflection on our personal relationship with each other. The 1973 Constitution Act had some powerful elements which were eroded by the 1976 Act. After some fourteen years, Tom King said: 'This legislation has failed'. The 1989 Act was put on the statute book principally because of the McBride Principles campaign in the United States; and at its first public outing before a tribunal in October of last year [1990], one of the most fundamental elements of the 1989 Act was found to be unworkable and is now being amended. We are therefore going to have (perhaps sometime this year) an amendment to the Act which was designed to amend the 1976 Act. That's not a good record, after fifteen years.

Bob Cooper:
Oliver and I disagree on quite a number of issues. I'm not going to take up the general points. I'll simply make one point, which is an

important point. Oliver points out the problem with the individual complaints. It certainly is a disaster, and we're going to put it right. But everybody who studies fair employment legislation has made the point that, in terms of bringing about change, the individual complaint side is the least important part. The individual complaint side is obviously crucially important from the point of view of the individual, but in terms of strategic change, it is not all that important. There are much more important parts of the legislation, such as the monitoring side, in terms of the ability to bring about change.

I would just make one other point, which is a worrying point. It concerns us that the statistics that we have show that the discrepancy in employment proportions in Northern Ireland is not actually caused by the 'bad guys'. It is not caused by the companies where Catholics are grossly under-represented. If you take all the 'bad guys' out, you'll find that, broadly speaking, there's a fairly good balance in employment representation, and that the real area where change has to take place is the discrepancy in unemployment figures. The area where real change is going to have to take place is where the company has 30% Catholics and should have 34% – a relatively small discrepancy. The good side of that is that those firms don't have to change all that much. The bad side is that it is much more difficult to bring about that sort of change. In some cases, it's easy to say what the company should do – where it's not getting any applications from the Catholic community, or it has other employment practices which are clearly discriminatory against Catholics. It's much more difficult to bring about change where there is a relatively small discrepancy; and that's something which faces all of us.

Curiously enough, if one looks to the United States, one of the big differences between our legislation and United States legislation is that, in certain instances, United States legislation permits preferential treatment. Those circumstances are circumstances where there is a gross disparity between the two sections (between blacks and whites). The wording of the Supreme Court is: where there is 'egregious discrimination' or where there is 'clear evidence of manifest imbalance'. They don't, in fact, tackle problems where there is a relatively small degree of under-representation. Possibly that is why the United States has not made any progress whatsoever in terms of rectifying the unemployment imbalances. It may be because they have been concentrating on the companies where there are 'egregious or manifest imbalances', rather than having to tackle in some ways the more difficult companies where there's a relatively small imbalance. That's the challenge that we have. To tackle the companies who say: 'We're not too bad'. And in a way, nobody can say they're too bad, where it's a matter of a relatively small under-representation.

Julie Cullen:
I don't know much about the legislation; but employers that I know, in the city centre and elsewhere, since the time the legislation was introduced, seem to be employing a token Catholic, a token Protestant. They're being brought in so that the employer will fulfil the requirements of the legislation. The employer can then say: 'I've made an effort'. But they're still discriminating in the workplace. I know of several instances of this, where people had to leave the job, because of the discrimination at work.

Bob Cooper:
I'd be very interested if you could come up with the names of those employers, because that's outrageous. As far as tokenism is concerned, all change has to start with tokenism. Our concern is that it doesn't end there. But if any employer thinks that by bringing in one token Catholic or one token Protestant they'll be satisfying us, they have another think coming to them.

Oliver Kearney:
But one token is sufficient where you do not have a strong affirmative action programme. And the legislation does not provide for strong affirmative action programmes.

Bob Cooper:
It does not provide for preferential treatment.

Oliver Kearney:
Nor does it provide for adequate goals and timetables to rectify community imbalances. It simply provides for the opportunity for everybody to apply for a job. It doesn't mean that they're entitled to get the job. There won't be any tie-breaker, as Tom Hadden pointed out. And the discretion as to what is 'fair and reasonable' in a given situation is still resting largely on the judgement of the employer.

On the question of the role individual complaints have to play, I don't think I'd let that one go, because the Equal Opportunities Commission, I believe, has succeeded in adopting, with slightly different legislation, an extremely vigorous role in pursuing individual cases of discrimination against women, and has implanted in employers' minds and in society at large a substantial change in attitude towards equality for women in employment; and I think that that has resulted partly from the EOC's capacity to become the representative of the complainant, to take the complaint on board and then to represent the complainant before a tribunal.

I have met two senior civil servants who have confirmed to me that when the 1989 Act comes up for review and amendment in about five years time, they anticipate that the legislation will have to be re-written to incorporate very strong affirmative action measures. They know that now. They know that today. They knew it when the 1989 Act was being written. And with all respect to Bob, the Civil Service has remained completely in control of the Fair Employment Commission, in relation to its budget, in relation to its policy-making, and in relation to the facility which the FEC has for exercising the sanctions available to it under the 1989 Act. If Bob decides that some employer should be registered as an unqualified person for the purpose of securing access to public contracts, it's within the capacity of the Civil Service department to override that for purposes of national security or in the public interest.

Bob Cormack:
The gender issue came up. Is it worth making any comment on that aspect of the problem, given that Catholic male unemployment is $2^{1}/_{2}$ times the Protestant rate, while for women it's $1^{1}/_{2}$ times. Catholic women's profile in employment doesn't look quite as bad compared to Protestant women as the Catholic male profile compared to the Protestant male profile. Does anyone want to talk about that aspect?

Joan McKiernan (Centre for Research on Women, University of Ulster):
Yes. I've been sitting here thinking about it, but you feel like you're intruding if you raise the gender issue. The legislation talks about equality, and the FEC report says that equality between Protestant and Catholic women seems OK; so women's equality is

OK. That was the impression given, that's what the headlines took up: that's that problem sorted out. When you look at government policy, government discussions, and the legislation, religion is the issue, and nothing else. We're not taking up the question of employment and unemployment, and the differences between male and female. I think it's not a separate issue, because it has a very direct effect upon altering the status of the Catholic working class, because of the kind of work, the levels of unemployment, the low wages coming into the Catholic working class, and the kinds of jobs that women are getting, as well as government policies.

No matter what the EOC does, it's good, but it's not going to have any impact. Nobody's talking about what kind of jobs are being brought in for people, including women, who are almost half the work-force at this point in time. What kinds of jobs are women getting? What kinds of projects is money being given to? What kinds of jobs are being created? If you go around the city centre, or you go around West Belfast, it's retail traps. Who works in shopping centres? It's women, part-time, on extremely low wages. And if it's only women getting those sorts of jobs, that means less money coming into the area, which increases the divisions between Protestants and Catholics.

In terms of the unemployment rates, the Government has made about twenty changes in the last few years, so that women are being wiped out of the count totally. So you're not even talking about women when you're talking about unemployment rates between the two communities in Northern Ireland, they're just not there. But they are more than half the population. An area that I'm particularly concerned with is training for women. And Britain (including Northern Ireland) is the worst for training courses in Europe.

Billy Hutchinson:
There was talk earlier about the money that's being pumped into West Belfast to create jobs. The working-class Catholics who work in the community will tell you that it isn't to create jobs. As far as they're concerned, it's more to destroy the name of Sinn Féin and to destroy the IRA. I tend to agree that that's what it's for. It isn't there to create jobs. If you look over the last four or five years, there haven't been any jobs created. The only thing there has been in there are the schemes that Father Matt talked about this morning. No real jobs have gone in. That's an argument that has

been brought forward by Catholic middle-class people: solicitors and doctors and people like that.

Julie Cullen:
The typical management committee in West Belfast!

Oliver Kearney:
There always was a Catholic middle class, in the sense that there was a professional tier who were servicing their own community. Their horizons have expanded economically and socially in the last twenty years. I think if the war in the streets were to end today, whatever about the Protestant section of the legal profession, the Catholic section of the legal profession would be decimated economically, because the provision of free legal aid means that the fees are available on the basis of a plea of guilty, regardless of the capacity of the individual to pay. The young fellow from the Shankill Road or the Falls Road is nothing more than a legal fee before the Diplock Court.

   Now, I don't mean to suggest that many Catholic lawyers are not working actively to try to protect the interests of their clients. But it is a fact that from the introduction of internment, and the fees associated with the Whitelaw tribunals, the Catholic legal profession mushroomed; and I think now represents close to 50% of the total legal profession. There has been an expansion into other areas, such as banking and the financial institutions, accountancy. But the main professional tier of the Catholic schoolteachers, the doctors, the lawyers – that tier still exists and has expanded, certainly in terms of the legal profession, in the last ten to fifteen years.

Arthur Green:
It's a pity David [McKittrick] is no longer here, because he was talking about the Malone Road, wasn't he? He seemed to have statistics to suggest that there was a really big electoral bloc in the Malone Road area of middle-class Catholics; and he was speculating upon whom they'd actually support in an election.

Paul Bew (The Irish Association; The Queen's University of Belfast):
I think this is one of the big questions. The thesis of David's article in the *Independent* is the major political miscalculation of the NIO,

who exaggerated the commitment of this Catholic middle class to devolution; and that it is the status quo, and the institutions of the status quo, that are more acceptable to this group. That, I think, is very interesting. Whether it's true or not, I'm not sure; but that's something we're going to find out about in a general election. It's one of the central questions in relation to economics and politics in Northern Ireland today.

Bob Cormack:
Perhaps it would be useful to talk about geographical differences. One of the criticisms that people made of that article was that this rising Catholic middle class may just be a Belfast phenomenon.

Bob Cooper:
I think Derry has a very strong, a very substantially expanding Catholic middle class. I don't think we should exaggerate. But if you take towns like Derry and quite a lot of other provincial towns, you'll find a substantial Roman Catholic middle class as well.

Paul Bew:
The 1911 census has, for the whole county of Antrim (which was then about 20% Catholic), two Catholic doctors. That gives you some idea of the transformation of society. There were sixty-seven Presbyterian doctors in county Antrim in 1911.

Kevin McCorry (Campaign for Democracy):
My interest in this topic goes back to the period when I was in the Civil Rights Association, and I came here today to try to discover why so little has been achieved. I think there is a fair agreement in this group that – to put it at its most charitable – there's a long road to go in relation to equality of opportunity, both in relation to gender (which was always a problem, and it's not peculiar to here) and in relation to the religious question. There's a long road to go; and quite honestly, Government to date hasn't proved its bona fides in relation to wanting to tackle that. I'm not saying that since 1972 direct rule has simply reproduced the old patterns. I'm saying that the legacy is so structurally deep in the society that Government has been, under certain pressures, prepared to do X, Y, and Z; but that X, Y, and Z have proved to be woefully inadequate to deal with the problem. So the problem continues to exist as a source of the continuing violence and instability in the

situation, and leads to the other responses by the state: that we have to maintain certain security measures and certain security policies, and we cannot do X, Y, and Z in relation to those, so it perpetuates the problem. That legacy remains, which hasn't been tackled.

Then there's the new level that has come on top of the problem; and I speak as one who believes that class is important in an analysis of the dynamic of a society, so don't get me wrong in relation to that. I would still believe fundamentally in class, in terms of understanding the dynamic of any society, and this society as all others. But on top of the class aspect, there is the question of what I would describe as the marginalized. I know the sociologists talk about the underclass. I think that's a wrong description, but I would describe them as the marginalized people in our society. They are the people in West Belfast – both in the Catholic areas and in the Protestant areas – who see themselves in relation to the state, be it the welfare system, be it policing, or whatever, as simply being at the receiving end of containment policies. They are contained within the areas, they are policed by their clergy through ACE schemes, through various organizations that are set up to massage statistics on unemployment, and all the rest of it. The main role of those organizations and schemes is to contain and to police those communities.

Paul mentioned the 1911 census in Antrim, and the two doctors. The more important thing in relation to Antrim today is this: in relation to the Northern Ireland Housing Executive, Antrim is a dumping ground for problem families. The housing estates in Antrim are a dumping ground, and the police's role in relation to those estates - and I know it as a solicitor – in terms of their attitude to the people in those areas, is what I would describe as essentially containment policies. So, on top of the layer of unresolved problems in terms of discrimination and inequality of opportunity, you have an additional source of contradiction and tension within the society. And quite frankly, the current sort of discussions, negotiations, about whether or not the SDLP will accept a devolved administration in Northern Ireland, or whether or not the Official Unionists will accept power-sharing – they may satisfy the particular interests of the political correspondents of the various newspapers, but the problems that are within the society are not being tackled. Nobody is tackling them. And until those issues are tackled, this place is going to be on the boil.

Bob Cormack:
Kevin, you're very skilful, like those skilful politicians, when they're being interviewed on radio or TV. They watch the clock and time their intervention so that they get the last word. Thank you all very much for your contributions.

EMERGENCY LEGISLATION AND THE ADMINISTRATION OF JUSTICE

Kevin Boyle (The British Irish Association; University of Essex):
The preliminary question is whether we could, as a democratic society, adequately respond to paramilitary violence without resort to any special legislative measures at all. There's a report coming out of New York quite soon by a very good organization called the Helsinki Committee, and one of the individuals on that committee, whom I met when they were over here, was playing around with the argument that Northern Ireland didn't actually need any special emergency powers at all, that you could cope with the emergency without resort to special powers of arrest and detention, with the ordinary courts in the ordinary way. So I think this is the first question: do people feel that the case is to be made that the reality of the scale of violence, and the fact that it has sustained itself for so long, does necessitate emergency measures? And that therefore, we should accept that and focus on how one safeguards against abuse in the use of those measures.

Robin Wilson (Editor of *Fortnight*):
I'm worried by the acceptance of this idea. First of all, it seems to me that the intellectual and moral onus is on people who want to have non-normal law to prove that that has to be so, because of all the ways that that is oppressive and undesirable. The second problem I have is that, inasmuch as there is non-normal law in Northern Ireland, all the evidence of history is that the security forces and the authorities want even more non-normal laws. And the third thing is that I do not see how we can possibly conceive of an end to the violence if our goal is not a progressive transition to a normal regime of law and civil liberties. If that's no longer our goal, then we have to accept the corollary of that, which is: we will always have terrorist violence. And I don't accept that corollary.

Kevin Boyle:
That was a widely held statement of aspiration. You didn't actually come down and say: 'Abolish the Emergency Powers Act, the Prevention of Terrorism Act **now**'; and that, in practical terms, we would be able to cope with the violence that we have at present within the existing arsenal of powers that there are in the ordinary law. You didn't quite say that.

Robin Wilson:
No, I'm saying that there should be a transition period. It's not a question of: 'Should we have the emergency laws or shouldn't we have the emergency laws?' What I am saying is: unless it's our goal, at the end of a transition period, to have no emergency laws, then we have to accept the corollary of that; and the corollary is that there will be terrorist violence. But I think we can, over a period of time, convert the current vicious circle of increasing authoritarianism, increasing terrorism, and therefore increasing demand for new measures, into a virtuous circle, beginning with the progressive winding down of emergency legislation.

William Smith (Justice for All, Belfast):
I'd like to support this last argument, because you either have justice or you don't have justice. And once you begin to accept emergency legislation as the norm, then you're compromising justice; and there's no way that I would accept that we should, in any way, compromise justice. The experience that we have in this country is that emergency legislation becomes the norm. I'll give an example of that, the Payment for Debt Act, which was introduced in 1972 under emergency legislation, after a rent and rates strike by a section of the community in Northern Ireland. Under that piece of emergency legislation, people who owed rent or rates or anything like that had it deducted from their wages or their benefits. That act was not repealed until a year ago, eighteen years after the strike was over. It was used throughout those eighteen years to extract repayment of debt from poor people. Once you begin to accept any level of emergency legislation, the end result is that it becomes a permanent feature rather than an emergency feature. And if the troubles in Northern Ireland were to stop today, the whole legal system would collapse, because over the twenty years, the courts and the administration within the courts –

the DPP and so on – have become totally dependent on emergency legislation. Emergency legislation has actually become the normal law.

Kevin Boyle:
What signal does the decision to make the Prevention of Terrorism Act (which is the UK-wide law, not the local Northern Ireland emergency law, but it also applies in Northern Ireland), what signal does making it permanent, albeit renewed on a five-year basis, give in this debate? My sense, living in Britain, is that there is an acceptance now of terrorism, not only Irish terrorism but the phenomenon of terrorism, as a new category of state concern, which has to be dealt with on a permanent basis.

Robin Wilson:
The trouble is that terrorism is seen like natural disasters. There's this thing in the world called terrorism; because it's a nasty old world we live in, isn't it? And this tends to lead people to adopt very common-sense conventional notions – all of which have one signal advantage: that is, that they avoid any responsibility on the part of the authorities for the fact that terrorism exists.

Terry O'Keeffe (University of Ulster):
The effects of the emergency legislation are very localized. William mentioned the Payment for Debt Act. That actually affected a small number of people and left a large number of middle-class people throughout the North of Ireland unaffected. The emergency legislation is exactly the same: it doesn't actually affect the majority of people in Northern Ireland. And therefore, increasingly, I think people have come to accept it – the occasional road block, getting their car searched, the sort of security in shops, and so on. We've learnt to live with that. Unless you live in certain areas, in which certain types of activity occur, you're not actually going to be affected by it. It becomes a background noise, if you like, and therefore doesn't have anything like the effect for the large majority of people in Northern Ireland that it does in areas like West Belfast, the Creggan, the Bogside, and so on.

William Smith:
It's all very well people saying: 'I don't mind my car being searched, I don't mind being stopped'. It's OK if they live in certain areas,

where you're only being stopped occasionally. If you lived in West
or North Belfast or any of the areas where there is the most
violence, then it becomes a wee bit tedious when you're stopped
maybe three or four times in the one day for the same thing –
checking your car, showing your licence – when it's already been
checked by the police three or four times.

Bill Webster (Rosemount Resource Centre, Derry):
The Establishment (or to give it its proper name, the ruling class
of Britain) have learnt certain lessons from the so-called troubles
here over the past twenty years, and they will not hesitate to apply
the experiences over here to Britain. On the question of putting
the Prevention of Terrorism Act onto the statute-book to apply to
the UK as a whole, what worries me is that other people who have
no connection whatsoever with terrorism can be caught up under
that legislation. I am one of those members of the labour movement who regularly paid visits to Britain when the Belfast/Liver-
pool ferry was on and was always stopped and held. I missed trains,
I missed connections, because, I believe, I was involved in trade
union activity, in socialist politics. I was held under that particular
legislation. So it's a nonsense for them to argue that that legislation has been introduced to protect society as a whole. We could
debate further whether that legislation is there to protect society
as a whole, or to protect private property and the state. But the
worrying thing is the number of people who are caught up under
that legislation who have nothing at all to do with terrorism.

Kevin Boyle:
I think we need to move on to the concept of the society we would
like to see, even if we can't actually deliver it at the moment; and in
terms of best democratic practice, the principle of emergency law
as being exceptional should be affirmed, and also economy in the
use of emergency powers. And that applies north and south. After
all, in the Republic, there's been emergency legislation since 1939
which has never been reviewed, scrutinized, or debated in over
fifty years. And arguably, best democratic practice would make
sure that the powers available are only the minimum needed, and
are not excessive.

The second thing that has emerged – which I suspect there will
be a fair consensus on too – is the issue of the role of security
policies. There is no means whereby the security policy can solve

our problem: that is to say, the violence is an outcrop from the political conflict in the community. The security policies can exacerbate or sustain, or can manage or inhibit the violence, but there is no solution for dealing with the violence, in the long term, other than political change. Our security supremos from time to time believe they've got **the** answer with particular policies. The reality is surely, after twenty years, that the violence has a political character; and fundamentally you cannot move to changing that without political accommodation.

Bernard Cullen (The Irish Association; The Queen's University of Belfast):
Could I offer one rider to that? In my experience, the military and security personnel I've spoken to at the higher level are never the ones who think they have the security solution. It's the politicians who, on the one hand, demand security solutions, and, on the other hand, from time to time claim that they have **the** security solution – 'Get into the ghettos and take out the terrorists'! I've never heard that kind of language from security chiefs. That only comes from politicians. And not just local politicians. It comes as well from the Michael Mates's of this world; and he really should know better, because of his military experience here. I think it's important to make that distinction: that many politicians over the years, in this debate between a security solution and a political solution, have consistently made matters worse, because of their facile demands for a security solution.

Kevin Boyle:
In some Latin-American societies, sustained attack on civil institutions, in which the military have been brought into a more direct role, has led in fact to the military becoming an alternative source of power, and ultimately to coups and take-overs. Is there any suggestion that as a result of the Northern Ireland experience the political muscle of the army is increased? Roughly what you're saying is that politicians shouldn't involve themselves in security matters; and that raises questions of accountability.

Bernard Cullen:
That isn't quite what I was getting at. My experience is that the security decision-makers are much more responsible and modest in their claims as to what security measures in themselves can

achieve. They don't make outlandish claims for what is possible through security operations. The security chiefs recognize that the violence here is an outgrowth of the political impasse. I don't have any worries whatsoever of the security chiefs running a political policy. I don't remember ever hearing Stormont Castle people making very great claims one way or the other about security either. It tends to be the politicians in the wings. I sometimes suspect that they're simply playing to the gallery here. Perhaps they really do believe that putting 30,000 troops into Andersonstown and the Creggan – a kind of Operation Motorman Mark 2 – will flush out the terrorists and bring an end to the terrorist problem. I can't believe that they actually do believe that. But that's the kind of thing they say from time to time.

I also think it's important that any politician who promises us a political solution which will bring an end to the terrorist violence is either deluding himself or is being irresponsible. My own view is that terrorism is no longer just an Irish thing, if it ever was just an Irish thing; it's a world-wide phenomenon. My sincere hope is that a political solution, acceptable to the vast majority of people in Ireland, will bring a radical diminution of terrorist activity. But really, it only needs half a dozen people to blow up Castle Court or St Anne's Cathedral, or St Peter's Cathedral. If we are realistic, there will always, in my view, be that handful of people who will want to express their political views through terrorism. But that should not panic us into having a vast panoply of emergency legislation indefinitely, to deal with that handful of people. I think we should have realistic goals: political progress which will radically diminish the number of terrorists, the degree of tacit support that terrorists need, the number of blind eyes that are turned to terrorists. If we can diminish that to a real minimum, in my view that is a really worthwhile ambition. But anyone who promises an end to terrorism – don't trust them. Because they can't deliver it.

Sammy Douglas (Seymour Hill Community Association, Dunmurry):
I think there are two sides to that argument. On the one hand, most people in Northern Ireland would say that there can't be a military solution on behalf of the British Government or on behalf of the British military force; but on the other hand, they wouldn't like to see a military solution on behalf of the republican movement or the loyalist movement. I welcome a statement recently in one of the

Southern newspapers, where Gerry Adams was interviewed, and he said that he didn't believe that the republican movement could win by military means. I think it's important to take those two strands and merge them together and say: 'There isn't any military solution. There must be some sort of political solution'.

Kay Lee (The Celtic Network, California):
I'm with the Celtic Network, which is based in California, near San Francisco. Regarding political solutions, it seems to us that if there is going to be a real political solution to the problems here, all parties must be included in the talks; and echoing what Desmond Tutu has said in Dublin, you can't have a democratic solution if you don't have a democratic representation of all the people whose lives are going to be affected. It seems unrealistic in the extreme to even propose such a non-solution.

Terry O'Keeffe:
You talked, Kevin, about inhibiting violence, or exacerbating violence, or stopping it. I think probably everybody believes there's no military way of stopping it or defeating it in that sense. I suspect that there's probably general agreement that military activity can easily exacerbate the violence. I think it would probably be far less easy to answer the question: How can we use military force – RUC, UDR, and so on – to inhibit violence? Do we do things like Coagh? Or do we search and arrest, and so on? And it's exactly there, I think, that lies the balance between legitimate inhibition – in stopping people killing, bombing, and so on – and exacerbating the situation.

When you think of the foundation of the UDR, and the killings of members of the UDR in Fermanagh and Tyrone, over the past number of years, and the extent to which that has now become a circle. People join the UDR because there seems, on their side, to be a republican campaign of genocide against Protestants; and yet, from the republican side, members of the UDR are legitimate targets. So I suppose we'll have to get on to the whole question of how you inhibit violence in a democratic society, even within emergency law.

William Smith:
When people talk about paramilitaries, everybody shies away. 'Paramilitary' becomes a dirty word. The paramilitaries are from the rank and file people. That's where they come from, they're not

some unknown quantity. They're not some sinister people sitting in the background. They're people from within our community, whom we work with, go to school with, maybe socialize with. It's now seventeen years since the politicians sat down and talked together, and we can see the charade they're having at the present time of talks about talks about talks. We can see the whole mess that **they're** making – not the paramilitaries. And yet the politicians hold the biggest brunt of the blame for the continuation of violence, because if there's no political solution there's a vacuum, and a vacuum is where the violence continues. Now, I'm not saying the politicians are totally to blame. What I'm saying is that there's nobody totally innocent, and there's nobody totally guilty. The politicians have a big responsibility for this violence. They can't just wash their hands like Pontius Pilate and say: 'It's not our fault, it's the paramilitaries, they're doing it all, and we're just politicians'. They are responsible for a lot of the trouble.

Tom Hadden (The Queen's University of Belfast):
On both sides, the paramilitaries are part of their community, and that's one of the reasons why we can't have a military solution. Depending on the political situation, we get huge numbers of loyalists coming forward and joining the UDA; and then it dies down, they think there's nothing to fight about or worry about. So that crisis blows over. And similarly, on the Catholic/republican side, it goes up and down, depending on feelings . . .

Bernard Cullen:
It goes up and down, very often, in direct response to actions of the security forces.

Kevin Boyle:
So we see the security role as ancillary, as assisting, or in some way holding the ground, while efforts are made to construct political solutions through dialogue. But what empirical or any other evidence is there that actions by the security forces serve as a recruiting sergeant to paramilitaries? Is that really only a statement of faith? How do we know?

Bill Webster:
For a start, from the Catholic point of view in Derry, Bloody Sunday directly led to a mass recruitment drive for the Provisional

IRA, as a direct result of the actions of the paratroopers on that day. So yes, there is a correlation between them: the blanket house-to-house searches, and that kind of military activity that goes on in the Catholic ghettos (as they're called). If unemployment is rising and the working class are getting the brunt of that, and factories are closing and benefits are being cut, and there's not enough public housing being built, you might think that in a so-called normal society, where democratic politics might prevail, that perhaps would lead to the building of a non-sectarian socialist organization. But in this country it doesn't happen. I'm not so sure what happens on the Protestant side; but what happens on the Catholic side is that that's the breeding ground for the recruitment drive into the IRA. There's no question about that.

Tom Hadden:
I think you can pin it down a little bit more precisely with respect to the backgrounds of people who come to court. Quite a large number of the people who come forward as active paramilitaries, certainly on the Catholic side, have had relatives shot. I think there's a lot of that; and that's why I mention the revenge element as being quite important as a ground for the security forces trying desperately to avoid shooting people dead.

Kevin Boyle:
There's an argument on the moral level, in terms of democratic theory, that one should obviously be constrained in the use of powers. But this is a practical perspective on it: that in fact the use of the emergency powers makes the problem more difficult, by recruiting new members to paramilitaries.

Robin Wilson:
There's some more subjective evidence, and that is the testimony of former or anonymously surveyed members of paramilitary organizations. The thing that comes up again and again and again in the classic books on the IRA is that the people interviewed all talk about some formative experience when they were young, which involved themselves or some person to whom they were close, whether family or friends, and some very unpleasant experience they had at the hands of the security forces. The phrase that comes up again and again and again in these testimonies is the desire to hit back, to fight back.

A second piece of evidence comes from Eamonn Mallie. In an interview he didn't use in his book, one Provo said to him: 'Repression we can cope with; but we find it hard to cope with reform'. If you look also at the way that the Provos have responded to the Anglo-Irish Agreement, it's been a bit like the scene in 'The Life of Brian', where the John Cleese character says: 'What have the Romans ever done for us?' And someone mentions the irrigation. And Cleese says: 'Apart from the irrigation, what have the Romans ever done for us?' Someone else mentions the sewage system. And Cleese says: 'OK, OK, apart from the irrigation and the sewage system, what have the Romans ever done for us?' And the whole way that the Provos have responded to the Agreement has been to say that the nationalist nightmare is still there; OK, there's this and there's that and there's the other, but the nationalist nightmare is still there. It's crucial to them to be able to say that not enough has been delivered on the reform side, that the emphasis has been so much on repression.

There's one final quite extraordinary bit of evidence. It doesn't concern actions by the security forces, but it's the same principle. I don't think we'd be here today if it weren't for Bloody Sunday, if it weren't for the way the hunger strikes were mishandled by the powers that be. And it's the same principle: you can go for repression or reform. As it happens, we've had reforms in the prisons, after all, in that basically the demands of the hunger strikers have now been granted; and the prisons are the source of no conflict at all. But there's a piece by Jim Gibney, who's a senior member of Sinn Féin, in a recent issue of *Republican News*, where he says quite openly that the republican movement was on its uppers in the late seventies, until the hunger strikes rejuvenated it.

Kevin Boyle:
Is there any other way of looking at that? Are we going to pass on and leave that as a consensus? That while no one is denying the need for a security response, the security policies that have been pursued have actually and avoidably prolonged and augmented the recruitment of paramilitaries.

William Smith:
From a Protestant point of view, in the Protestant ghettos one of the biggest recruiting agents for the paramilitaries was the like of political decisions rather than military decisions, such as the

Sunningdale Agreement with its Council of Ireland, and the Anglo-Irish Agreement, which has resulted in a response from the Protestant community. As well as that, obviously, IRA violence. When people were killed or blown up during 1972, for example, the Protestants who had relatives or friends blown up obviously responded to that situation. So it's probably slightly different within the Protestant communities.

Sammy Douglas:
From a Protestant community myself, like Billy I see it from two different strands. First of all, you've got the over-activity of the security forces; and also the Anglo-Irish Agreement. Certainly, in some of the areas I've worked in as a community worker, Protestants were victims of that over-activity. But also I think that the under-activity of the security forces, especially in the seventies, led to the recruitment of mass numbers of working-class Protestants into some of the paramilitary forces, because as they saw it (and still do see it), if the forces of law and order are not protecting the law-abiding citizens, then there must be some other form of activity that people like this could get involved in to protect their families.

I was born in Sandy Row, and many of the people in Sandy Row that I knew who ended up in the likes of the UDA, the UVF, the Red Hand Commandos, or whatever – many of those people were ordinary people. I don't think they were very sectarian, but they saw a real threat to their lives and to their families. Some of them were business people. I knew one man who was from the church: he was called the padre of the UDA in Sandy Row. So for many of those people it was a genuine response, but over the years the activities got more and more extreme.

Kevin Boyle:
This is obviously another dimension to add to the picture we're drawing. It's not a question of a single community and the problems of dealing with the violent challenge from that community. We're talking about both communities, which adds another level of complexity to the working through of security policy.

Jean Murray (St Mary's College, Belfast):
Is this not putting the security forces in a no-win situation? The way this discussion has developed, have we not actually put the

security forces in an impossible situation? If they adopt these particular policies in the nationalist/republican areas, then they're going to be a recruiting agent for the IRA. But if they **don't** do that, then they're going to have the loyalist community joining paramilitaries. What can they do to do it right?

William Smith:
I don't think that's what's being said here. I would like to make it particularly clear that repression in Northern Ireland or repression in the South happens to both Protestants and Catholics; and people, particularly Catholics, must get away from the rhetoric or the myth that Protestants are better off than them, because I've spoken to many people on the Falls Road, and they have the same opinion as me: that the people on the Shankill Road are no better off economically – either jobs-wise or as housewives – than the people on the Falls Road. We must get out of that rhetoric. Where there was discrimination, let's be honest about it and say there was discrimination, both North and South. We talk about IRA hunger-strikers dying. De Valera let them die in 1937–39, long before Maggie Thatcher was around. And there's still emergency legislation on the books there from 1939.

So let's be honest about the thing. Protestant people suffered as much under emergency legislation as the Catholic people did. Supergrass trials affected Protestants the same as it affected Catholics. In fact, more Protestants were arrested under supergrass trials. Internment affected Protestants the same as it affected Catholics. All those repressive laws that were applied in Northern Ireland were applied on both sides with equal vigour. The policemen didn't turn round and say: 'Are you a Protestant or a Catholic, before I hit you over the head with a baton?' It happened on the Protestant side too.

So we're not calling for repressive legislation; in fact, the reason I'm here is because I'm fighting against repressive legislation. And regarding lethal force, Protestants historically did not criticize the state because they felt that if they did so they were being disloyal. They acquiesced, if you like, in the repressive laws that were being implemented. We have at least seven cases of loyalists who were shot dead by the security forces. But these cases have never been taken up, because we have nobody on our side. None of our unionist politicians will criticize the security forces about the shoot-to-kill policy. Brian Robinson is the latest case. There were loyalists being shot dead throughout the early eighties. Their inquest lasted five minutes, and that was it. There was no more said about it. Lethal force is applied to both communities.

Kevin Boyle:
I'd like to say a little bit about context there, if I may, since I'm quite interested in this issue of lethal force. If we again take our Latin-American parallel, one's looking at the phenomenon of arbitrary killings by the state forces: that is to say, people being shot without any justification, where they could have been arrested. You get a situation where, in those conflicts, the vast majority of people who are killed are civilians, and the author of those killings is the security system.

Northern Ireland has this very considerable difference: the bulk of the killings have been by paramilitaries of civilians, not by the legitimate authorities, as it were. And secondly, the security forces are themselves the second largest category of casualties in this twenty-year conflict, which again distinguishes the situation from other conflicts in the world. This is not to diminish the problem, but to focus it: the security forces have been responsible for something like 13–14% of the deaths since the early 1970s. But is it true – this is the issue that Tom Hadden raised – that the laws are inadequate to control or to make accountable the police and the security forces?

Bernard Cullen:
With your permission, before we get on to lethal force, I'd like to make one point. It has struck me over the years that in terms of recruiting support for paramilitaries – not recruiting actual paramilitary operatives, but for recruiting the thousands of people who are prepared to turn a blind eye and give tacit support – it's not the lethal force that's the most important factor, it's the humdrum, minor, day-to-day, petty harassment. Jean asked earlier: 'What are the security forces to do?' What they have to do is find a balance. For the past twenty-odd years, I've been constantly frustrated by the stupidity of the actions of the security forces. Day in, day out; not the few dramatic cases that hit the headlines three or four times a year.

You asked for evidence earlier. I've plenty of anecdotal evidence. My mother lives in Andersonstown. I live in the comfort and security of Belfast 9. I drive in my car to visit her regularly, through security road-blocks on Kennedy Way. I'm very seldom stopped. I wear a nice suit, a tie, and so on. If I am stopped, I'm invariably treated courteously. In recent years, our teenage son has begun to drive his own car to visit his grandmother, across Balmoral Avenue and Kennedy Way. Here we have an 18/19-year-old in his old banger. If there is a road-block, not only do they never fail to stop him, but they usually abuse him, get him out of the car, and generally push him around. Now luckily enough he's an intelligent young man. The irony of this is that this was going on while he was being trained to govern the empire as a pupil of the Royal Belfast Academical Institution!

But the more important point is: if it's happening to him, it's happening all the time to the young fellows – most of them unemployed – who actually live in Andersonstown. I hear it all the time from my own brothers and sisters. Day in, day out, young people in working-class areas are being gratuitously, senselessly, needlessly messed about, harassed; and many of them are not going to make the same level-headed response that my son makes; and that we in this room would make.

So it seems to me that that has to be addressed. There seems to be a serious lack of training, a lack of policy being passed down the line. I don't believe that squaddies cannot be trained; that constables cannot be trained, no matter how difficult the circumstances, to be courteous, and not to have the silly idea that the terrorists only drive around in bangers and don't wear ties. That's the level of stupidity at which they operate, and it's a serious on-going problem.

Noel Sinnamon (Ulster Quaker Peace Committee):
Are we saying that an army is an unsuitable instrument to deal with the public in civil disturbances?

Kevin Boyle:
Well, it may be unsuitable, but what we established before is that we have no other option, given the nature of the security problems.

Noel Sinnamon:
But it seems clear to me that the police have a different approach: they use the minimum of force. It seems very hard to me that the young men in a force like the army are trained in one certain way,

which gives them victories in places like the Falklands and so on, and suddenly they're thrown into Northern Ireland and all their policies have suddenly been reversed. It seems to be asking an awful lot of a sergeant, a lieutenant, and the squaddies. We really should be looking at the training of police to handle the emergency situation.

John Ledlie (Northern Ireland Office):
I think that's a very important and relevant point. I think you could say that in Northern Ireland today – 1991 as opposed to 1971 – we are asking the army to carry out really quite significantly different duties in many parts of Northern Ireland than was the case at the beginning of the troubles, different from what their training accustoms them and trains them to do. But your point, mister chairman, is a very valid one: what alternatives are there? We might want to explore that, I think. And I wouldn't at all disagree with what Bernard was saying, that there obviously is scope for doing more in attempting to refine practice. But at the same time, I do think we need to bear in mind the nature of the organization with which we're dealing; and in a sense what you're talking about is really asking them to carry out policing jobs; and in many cases, really very sensitive and socially refined activities, which it's hardly fair and indeed inappropriate to ask them to carry out.

William Smith:
I accept that the squaddies from all parts of England, Scotland, and Wales don't join the British army to come over here to fight for the British Government; they join the army in most cases because they've no job. So I accept what he was saying about the army. Now we come on to the RUC. You can't expect the army to do the policing, if the RUC don't do the policing. The biggest problem in the like of West Belfast and North Belfast is that the RUC hand over control to the paramilitaries.

To give you an example: there was a shop broken into, burgled, and some of the stuff that was stolen was left round in an empty house beside me. One of the neighbours alerted me to this; so I went over and saw it was from the shop. So I phoned up the police, and the police came out. This was May 1988. And the policeman said to me: 'That's OK. There'll be a detective out to see you within the next few weeks'. I'm still waiting on that detective coming! I'll give you another instance. Last summer, during the very hot weather, some vandals on the Shankill estate had actually broken the fire hydrants, and the water was gushing all over the place. They actually smashed so many that the water pressure went down, and old people on the Shankill estate couldn't even get water out of their taps. I phoned up the police and asked them about it, and the police told me to go down and see the UDA.

That is a fact. It happens in republican areas too, because the RUC is totally geared to fight the war against terrorism. They have no facilities whatsoever to tackle the ordinary issues of burglaries and petty crime in these communities; and then in turn the people turn to the paramilitaries for help. And this is why knee-capping becomes a popular thing among the people. This is why paramilitaries can get away with it for years, kneecapping people and meting out that sort of justice, because the RUC fail to do the policing job they're supposed to do. Now whether that can be tackled by having a community police force or a paramilitary police force, I don't know; but certainly the police have abdicated their responsibility of dealing with crime in those areas.

Ann McCann (The Peace People, Belfast):
I work with the Peace People, and I live in West Belfast, up near Suffolk. I just wanted to reiterate what William said: it's just exactly the same in West Belfast.

William Smith:
I **am** from West Belfast – Protestant West Belfast! Some people tend to forget.

Ann McCann:
In the part of West Belfast that I live in, not only do the police give you instructions to go to Sinn Féin, but as often as not the operation is actually successful, people do get their property back. Jobs that you would have gone years ago to the police with, people take it for granted now that you do not call the police. The only times you call the police now are if somebody has died or if you happen to be insured and you have to inform the police. So there's a total lack of trust; and I think that that comes down to one big issue, and that is, that people perceive the police as being above the law. In other words, if the police overstep the law with them, people have no means of bringing them to task.

Colin McClure (Fisherwick Presbyterian Church, Belfast):
We've got to remember also that the police have a particular
community situation to work within. In a sense, violence brutalizes
all of us. If you take a young constable out of the training centre
and you send him to Derry or up to the border, where there are
people spitting at him, where there are old ladies calling him
names, and then you send him back to Belfast to the centre of
town, where people are asking him the time and asking directions.
Now, is it not unreasonable to expect a young fellow to make that
sort of transition without some sort of reciprocal transition on the
part of our community? How can you expect a young fellow of
average intelligence to work in West Belfast with people who may
be spitting at him and calling him names; and also with people
who are prepared to give him the time of day?

Ann McCann:
If he can't do that, he shouldn't be in the police; he should be
trained to do it.

Colin McClure:
But it goes beyond spitting in his face. You're dealing with young
men – and indeed, young women – who are anticipating that
around the corner somebody might be waiting to shoot them.
Now, surely there's got to be some reciprocal gesture on the
community's part?

Robin Wilson:
If I could reply to something John Ledlie said: we're not talking
about refining something here; we're talking about a really serious
problem. We're talking about the fact that it takes more than two
years to get the police to deal with a burglary. It's taken five years
and more since the issue of accompaniment of UDR patrols by the
RUC was first mentioned in a communiqué following the first
meeting after the signing of the Anglo-Irish Agreement. Nothing
has ever been done about it. Looking across Northern Ireland as a
whole, it is clear that the UDR is the single biggest source of
antagonism and antipathy on the part of Catholics in Northern
Ireland because of its frequently appalling behaviour – which I
have experienced personally.

The second thing is, I think there are people like Dr Daly, for
example, who has made quite a big effort to try and meet the RUC

halfway, and that is valuable. The situation here is a bit like when there was an uprising in East Berlin in 1953, and a statement was put out by the officially-sponsored Writers' Union, which said that the Government had completely lost confidence in the people; and Bertolt Brecht said, 'well, we'll just have to elect a new people'. It's not up to the people to support a police force, it's up to a police force to be able to win the support of the people. That's where the onus lies.

Kevin Boyle:
Do you take the point that it would be helpful if the community could take cognizance of the dilemmas facing the police as well? They're being pulled in two directions: there's their civilian role and there's the reality of the violence.

William Smith:
I would say: what about the young policeman with his baton, his handcuffs, his flak jacket, his rubber bullet gun, and his machine gun? Not the one that the reverend was talking about, but the guy that comes out and he's looking for a bit of action. Geared up to the teeth like Rambo, and he goes up the Shankill where people aren't shooting at the police. At the time of the signing of the Anglo-Irish Agreement, when there was rioting on the Shankill Road, the police were in their landrovers, shouting out at the kids and firing rubber bullets out at them. Let's be honest. The police force is not capable of the situation because they're not trained in the situation. Most of them join because they can't get a job anywhere else. They get a couple of months of a crash course, and then they're thrown out into West or North Belfast with all this gear. But if you phone up about your house being broken into, they won't even come out. They won't even investigate. That's not a myth, that's a fact.

Sammy Douglas:
I'd like to get back to the whole question of harassment. I don't think the UDR or the army have a monopoly on harassment. I think the police are part of that whole equation. I work in East Belfast and I work with community workers all across Belfast; and certainly there seems to be real disrespect for the police among the Protestant community, particularly the young, because of the way the police have harassed people in the Protestant areas. So I

don't think that harassment is exclusive to nationalist/republican areas, it also applies to areas like East Belfast and the Shankill. It's a major problem, particularly since the Anglo-Irish Agreement, that the people in Protestant areas have lost respect for the police.

Noel Sinnamon:
There are certainly a lot of complaints about the police not being active. But it's not necessarily true across the board. I live in a predominantly Protestant area, but the shops next to me are predominantly Catholic. They're broken into quite often, and invariably the police respond very quickly. The police obviously know that these are Catholic shops, and they've been very co-operative.

Ann McCann:
It depends on the area.

Kevin Boyle:
It's interesting that there has been no suggestion of a sectarian dimension in the matter of where the police do and do not operate satisfactorily. The question here is one of priorities, whether burglaries would be investigated; and I assure you that in parts of London a similar problem arises.

Bill Webster:
That brings us back to the whole question of normal policing. What's meant by 'normal policing'? My understanding of police forces world-wide is that they've always been involved in shoot-to-kill policies. Members of the so-called security forces have always infiltrated workers' organizations and other organizations, they've always had *agents provocateurs*, they've always had a murky hand in the most mysterious killings that have taken place, particularly with a political connotation.

I don't believe there's normal policing here. Of course, on the surface, everything can appear to be rosy: going up the motorway, you might see a cop pass you on a motor bike, and you say: 'There's the M1 policeman on traffic duty'; you might see a policeman helping an old lady across the road; you might see a policeman calling to a house where there's been a fire, to assist the fire brigade. But that's not the role of the police in Northern Ireland. The role of the police in Northern Ireland is a direct reaction to the overall political or terrorist activity that is taking place. That is primarily what they are employed for.

But the point is, this situation is not unique to us. Maybe I don't read as much as other people in this room do, but I do go through the daily press. I defy you to name me one country on this planet where there is contentment, where there is confidence, where there is security amongst people, in relation to the police force. There's not one. From east to west – there's not one. And in my home town of Liverpool now, there is actually uproar, in Bootle and elsewhere, because of the rampages the police have been going on. And there are no IRA cells in Bootle – at least, not that we know of. It's just putting the boot into the poor, putting the boot into the young people. I think Bernard was right when he said that you look in vain if you look to the present-day politicians for a solution to the problems here.

I'm reminded of the famous Leak 37, the document that the Provisional IRA got hold of. That document was an assessment of the current military activity here, drawn up by military strategists, and I agree with them. They were correct, because they said, on the one hand, they could not win militarily, and on the other hand, neither could the Provos; and it took Adams years to come to that realization. And what they warned against was that as long as the social conditions endured in Northern Ireland, and especially if those social conditions deteriorated, there could be a political movement outside of the control of the IRA, or its sister organizations on the Protestant side, leading to a united political movement of working people; and that was the danger as far as they were concerned. So the military chiefs were not primarily concerned with a pure military solution, but were warning these stupid politicians of the dangers that lay ahead.

Kevin Boyle:
I've read that document as well, and I followed you halfway along. But I don't recall them warning or giving signals that a united working class was something that politicians should be concerned about.

Jean Murray:
I would just like to take stock of the point that we have got to in this discussion. On the one hand, we started out on this particular train of thought, which I think was instigated by Noel, talking

about the unacceptability of squaddies coming over to Northern
Ireland and being expected to do a job which they hadn't been
trained to do; and it seemed that everybody assented to that
particular view at that stage of the discussion. Now, it seems to me
that if you accept that, then the only people who are able to do the
job are the RUC; which means you've got to learn to live with the
RUC being in flak jackets, with rubber bullet guns and whatever
else. You can't have it both ways!

William Smith:
I accept what Jean said, to a certain extent: the police are in a
difficult position. But it's how they behave in the different situations which counts. I'll give you an example. A few months ago, on
the Shankill Road, a fight started outside a Chinese carryout. The
police came to intervene, and a row started between the police
and the young lads. Then the batons started being drawn, and
more of the kids got involved until you had something like a mini-
riot outside the Chinese. And the police then used rubber bullets.
     That is what I'm talking about. You can't have a situation where
the police can use these rubber bullets just whenever they feel like
it. The rubber bullet gun was designed for political riots, where
there were thousands of people involved. They were not designed
for domestic use. We must have a distinction between domestic
violence and paramilitary violence or terrorism. And the police
apply the same tactics to both. And that is why the police are no
longer acceptable in the Protestant community – I'm talking about
in the inner city, in the like of the Shankill Road, Sandy Row, East
Belfast. I'm not saying it's the RUC's fault as a force; but the
individual people within that force are not distinguishing between
domestic violence and terrorism. They apply the same tactics to
both.

Bernard Cullen:
I think we've all agreed now that the real problems of police/
community relations are in specific areas: that they're not throughout Northern Ireland, they're in working-class areas, in the poorer
areas. Where I'd like to take issue with some of the language that
Billy and others have been using, is with respect to statements such
as: 'The police are not supported in Protestant working-class areas'. I don't know the Shankill. But I do know Andersonstown and
the Falls fairly well. What we mustn't lose sight of is the fact that

Andersonstown and other nationalist working-class areas contain a whole range of attitudes to the police.

I don't think we should go down this desperately pessimistic road, that it's the police on the one side, with their batons and guns and rubber bullets, and on the other side a united opposed working-class community. It's just not like that. And that's what makes it even more frustrating, to get back to my anecdote about petty harassment. My suspicion, based on twenty-odd years of talking to people, is that the majority of people in Andersonstown do support the police, want to support the police more effectively, and want the police to support **them**. That's where the police have to seize upon their allies in the community, and that's where they're failing up until now.

Kevin Boyle:
No doubt we'll come back to this question after lunch, because it's a very interesting issue. We've been told that in housing and other areas of social provision, the 's' word is no longer relevant; that they're no longer sectarian issues. Sectarianism has not been mentioned here, and I'd like to come back to that after lunch, and examine whether it is somehow a past category in describing the problem.

Robin Wilson:
Before we break, I'd just like to back up entirely what Bernard has just said about the police. I only wish the RUC understood the degree to which a lot of the problem in West Belfast is just because the police do not behave like a police force. The people actually want to support them, they want them to behave like a police force, and they can't understand why they won't; and that really frustrates them.

The second thing is back to Jean's point. I would take Jean's point if it was the case that, well, it's unfortunate, but this is the only way to do it, we have to have these guys armed to the teeth because that's the only way it can be done. But I think it's the contrary to that. It's not as if being armed to the teeth and operating in an associated way actually brings good policing either. It tends to lead to a certain kind of style and manner which is very well chronicled in John Stalker's book: a certain set of attitudes and approaches, which not only militates against good policing, but actually leads to very bad policing.

The corollary of that world of special squads and of macho policing is, as John Stalker found, extraordinary inefficiency in the force. Incredible inefficiency that goes unchallenged, because people say: 'We can't criticize the police force because too many of them have got killed', and so on. No one is saying that the police shouldn't have the right to have defensive protection of all sorts, whether it's flak jackets or whatever it is – that's not the issue. The issue is how they behave in their day-to-day dealings with people.

[LUNCH BREAK]

Kevin Boyle:
Before we leave the general question that we were dealing with before lunch, about attitudes to the security forces and the dilemmas facing the military forces and the police, let me remind you of the question I posed towards the end of the last session: is the sectarian dimension to law enforcement something that's no longer an issue in those terms? Bernard reminded us, in his introductory remarks this morning, that one doesn't talk in terms of a sectarian dimension any more when one is talking about housing and other social provision. When we talked this morning about policing, I noted that people were using universal categories: we were talking about the relationship between young people in inner cities and styles of policing; we were talking about priorities in policing, that they've no time to investigate burglaries because they're dealing with the war, as it was put.

But no one raised the question of the police force as it was perceived in the past – and as many people believed it was in fact – namely, an instrument of the Unionist party, mobilized by bigotry. Are all of those categories gone? Is sectarianism relevant in the police force today? Do people think that Catholics are policed differently than Protestants, by reason of their religion? Or is the perception of the RUC in the minority community, as a partisan police force, irreversible? That is to say, that one could never contemplate, even in the situation of a return to normality, that the RUC would get sufficient recruits from the minority community to be an effective, acceptable police force for the whole community.

Robin Wilson:
First, there is no doubt that the UDR is a blatantly sectarian force. In that sense Lord Hunt was absolutely right, when he wrote, in a

letter to *The Independent* about a year ago, during the debate about collusion, that he felt that there really was no longer any possibility you could reform the UDR. Much of that applies to the RUC. It is certainly still seen as a sectarian force, and there's plenty of evidence for that view in the John Stalker book. There's been no serious inquiry into the RUC, its operation, its accountability, its effectiveness, and so on, since 1970; and that's appalling.

The only one there's been is the one that happened almost by accident, the Stalker book. And that was a damning indictment of the routinely sectarian culture that he came across. For example, there was the episode when he tried to talk to Pat Finucane, the lawyer who was later assassinated, in a corridor in the law courts. Some constable came up to him and said to him: 'What are you doing? That man's an IRA man'. And Stalker came across that kind of thing, just over and over again. I don't think that the RUC case is as bad as the UDR; the UDR is a lost cause. I think the RUC can be reformed. But I wouldn't say it's not seen as sectarian.

Kevin Boyle:
Before we leave the question of structures, would anyone like to say anything about the new independent police complaints machinery?

Tom Garrett (Independent Commission for Police Complaints):
We certainly do try, as an organization, to enlist the aid of the local community at grassroots level; and as a relatively new organization we are making continual contact with the community on both sides of the divide and informing them of our role. I think myself, as a relative new boy on the Commission, that under James Grew it's doing very good work in trying to disseminate the notion that we are one of the very few bodies in the world in which independent civilians have oversight of complaints against the police. There is a great deal of publicity, I think, still to be done on its behalf, but we are going ahead with that. We're getting into schools now, in West and East Belfast, and informing young people of our role. We're inviting community groups into HQ of the Commission; and I think myself that a lot of very good work is being done by a body which is certainly seen to be independent.

Ann McCann:
As a member of the public, I hope that that would be the case, but I certainly don't think that the public would see it as an

independent body. You can have good PR, you can get into schools and talk to both sections of the community; but the only way that it'll be perceived as a credible body is when people see results. And so far there haven't been any. And until the public at large see that, they won't look upon it as an independent body.

Tom Garrett:
Could I ask what you mean by results?

Ann McCann:
Well, when someone is accused of overstepping his job as a policeman or a UDR soldier or whatever, that they actually see him convicted – not only charged and then allowed to go free or whitewashed, but that he serves time like anybody else.

Tom Garrett:
Well, I would refer you to the statistic published in our recent report that we investigated last year nearly 900 cases, and some 13% of them resulted in some form of action against officers in the RUC, ranging from criminal charges to disciplinary action, depending on the gravity of the offence. That, I think, does speak for itself to some extent.

Ann McCann:
I'm just talking as a member of the public; but certainly, people do not read these reports. We were told by the Chief Constable, when we went to the police station, that we should read his report to see what disciplinary action had been taken. But if people break the law in any other job, they don't just lose their job; they go to the courts and then they serve time. And I think it's perceived by the public that when the police do break the law (exactly as you said there) they're disciplined and maybe lose their jobs. But as far as I'm concerned, I don't think that that's enough. If they've broken the law, they have to face the courts like everybody else.

Tom Garrett:
Well, in some cases, I assure you they do.

Jean Murray:
Can I just raise an issue with regard to structure that I think is important? And I'm speaking here as a former member of the

Police Authority. If we are going to have structures that are going to gain the confidence of the community, then those structures have to be representative. That includes the police service, which means we need Catholics to come along and join the RUC. We also need the political representatives of the Catholic community to sit on bodies like the Police Authority. And until they accept that responsibility, and until they are prepared to work within the structure for the kind of independent oversight that Tom Garrett was talking about, then things won't change.

Now, I think there's a real contradiction here: on the one hand, we have this discontented Catholic community that Robin was talking about, who yet have no representation at any formal party level on the bodies, like the Police Authority, that have been established to be involved in oversight. It's a pity that there are no politicians here today. It's a pity that the SDLP, for instance, aren't here to listen to the discussion that we are having, because the story we have heard today is one of even-handed policing. It may be policing that you don't particularly like, but everybody seems to agree that it's being administered even-handedly. Perhaps were they to hear that, then that might change that party's perverse stance with regard to membership of structures like the Police Authority, which they have so far refused to participate in.

Kevin Boyle:
As Ann was saying, people don't read reports. But they do hear about killings, so perhaps, in the short time left, we really should touch on that substantive dimension of Tom's presentation this morning.

I wonder if a way into this question of shootings is the training question: one of the arguments put forward this morning was that it's not surprising that soldiers fire first and think later. That's what they're trained for: they're trained to kill. Some other military forces on the Continent, for example, which are more evidently involved in civilian work, over the years have devised policies of shooting in the air and other measures for the use of firearms. Whereas the British approach for soldiers is: you shoot to kill, if you shoot at all. All the controls are at the point where you stop the soldier from using the gun. But once the gun is discharged, then you aim for the largest mass of the body and you continue firing until you're told to stop firing. Is that a part of the problem: that soldiers in fact are dealing with these situations as a

military operation, and yet they're being judged by civilian standards, and therefore there's an outcry?

Noel Sinnamon:
Certainly, the Ulster Quaker Peace Committee believes very strongly
that the army is an unsuitable instrument to use in areas of civil
unrest; and it has been our policy for years that the army should be
progressively withdrawn and replaced by a civilian police force,
preferably drawn from across the religious divide. I can't believe
that it's realistic to have two sets of conduct for young soldiers –
one of maximum force in wartime, and then every time they do a
tour of duty in Northern Ireland, to suddenly have those policies
reversed and expect those young men to do something that's
totally against their training and use minimum force. I think that
as a community we should be asking for the withdrawal of the
army from Northern Ireland.

Kevin Boyle:
I would like us to spend a little time on the issue of incidents where
people are shot – whether they are paramilitaries or not. The
argument, as we heard this morning, is that the rules are such that
it's possible for them to allow for a lawful ambush: that intelligence is available that IRA people are going to be engaged in
some act of terrorism, and the opportunity is there for these
people to be dealt with differently other than being killed, but
they're killed. That's the accusation.

Bernard Cullen:
Could I ask Tom to elaborate on that phrase that he used this
morning, which mystified me somewhat, about the possibility of
interpreting the legal rules in such a way that lawful killing could
be planned.

Tom Hadden:
I think that's right. I think there have been circumstances in which
I certainly suspect, though I couldn't prove, that operations have
been set up, in which the instructions given – either overt or nods
and winks – are that there'd be no harm if these people ended up
being shot dead.

Bernard Cullen:
But what's the role of the yellow card then?

Tom Hadden:

There are little bits of the yellow card which I find objectionable. The section in relation to joy-riding (section 5a(3)) appears to authorize shooting joy-riders. There's section 5b, which I also find objectionable, which is in relation to shooting people who have just committed an act but are no longer presenting a danger to anybody. But generally speaking, the yellow card is OK. The difficulty is in ensuring that the yellow card is actually applied. And there have been a number of occasions in which, without having access to the evidence (which brings us on to the inquest), I have suspicions that the yellow card rules have not been applied. In other words, people have been shot, when it wasn't strictly necessary in order to preserve life; which is the international test and the yellow card test.

People have been shot, but it has proved impossible to bring prosecutions, because the other important element, which is Section 3 of the 1967 Criminal Law Act, says you may use such force as is reasonable in the circumstance; and the legal interpretation of that is a good deal wider than the yellow card. And that means that when the case goes up to the DPP, all he can say is: 'It may be in breach of the yellow card, but I can see absolutely no chance of a successful prosecution under Section 3 of the Criminal Law Act, therefore I direct no prosecution'. And as the law is that it's murder or nothing, it's nothing.

It's that complicated relationship of yellow card, Section 3 of the Criminal Law Act, the murder/manslaughter rule, that results in no sanction. We're trying to persuade the authorities that really you must do something about this, because otherwise we will continue to have lethal shootings, we will continue to refer the cases to the DPP, and the DPP will continue to have to say: 'In all honesty, I cannot prosecute these people, because they are 90% likely to be acquitted'.

Kevin Boyle:

And just to add a footnote to that: it's possibly inevitable, but it contributes to the extent to which this problem corrodes confidence, that the DPP himself does not think it appropriate to give reasons as to why he doesn't prosecute. So you end up with a situation where, by reason of the nature of the operation, certain rules can be justified independently. There is, on the face of it, no answer in the public domain to what the propagandists would argue is a police murder or an army murder, except that the matter is with the DPP, or there will be an inquest.

Robin Wilson:

To add to our worries about the yellow card and the limitations of the legislation and the DPP's failure to give reasons, is the whole sequence of judgements that have been given over the years. There have been some unbelievable judgements. We've had judges saying things like: 'If you go out in a posse in the Wild West ...'; 'You can't apply a jeweller's scales to these situations'; and talking about 'sending people to the final court of justice'. It's not very hard to see how even moderate sections of the Catholic community in the North find such judgements unbelievable. And they have created a climate in which it would be a very perverse-minded soldier who thought that they were likely to join Private Thane as the one member of the regular army to be found guilty of murder.

Kevin Boyle:

Not denying that they are necessary as part of the reality of the situation, the use of firearms by the security forces is an issue that should be addressed from the point of view of best practice. Anyone want to bring up the post-shooting dimension which Tom touched on? Whether the institution of the inquest is adequate to deal with the need for some sort of reassurance that rules are being applied properly and that the enforcers are subject to the same rules as they themselves are enforcing.

John Ledlie:

Some of these are indeed quite technical legal questions. I would entirely accept that what we have described today as the use of lethal force by agents of the state, by the security forces, is an extremely important and topical and appropriate question to address. I think all of us as citizens need to ensure that when such measures are exercised, they are exercised with extreme care, and in circumstances which we are all, as members of a democratic society, aware of and conscious of and able to scrutinize as best we can.

That said, it is a very difficult and sensitive area to get into easily. Tom Hadden is absolutely right to describe the circumstances under which the Director of Public Prosecutions (who is an entirely independent agent, I hasten to add) decides whether a prosecution should be brought or not, on the grounds of whether the circumstances brought to him are likely to result in a successful prosecution. And in the cases and the circumstances you've described, Tom, there will be few cases where those criteria will be met. And that is absolutely a valid question to debate, as to whether those legal criteria, which allow the DPP to have a good chance of bringing a successful prosecution, should actually be changed. That's a perfectly genuine issue, which people can and should debate, and which Parliament might indeed want to look at at some stage.

I think one also needs to bear in mind the point that came up this morning, which was what I would describe as the public confidence aspect of the exercise of lethal force, which is very much what I would describe as a double-edged sword. Because there are certain people in the community (and we all know who they are and we could see them on television over the last week or so) who would regard the exercise of lethal force in circumstances such as Coagh a few days ago as entirely appropriate, and indeed as much to be welcomed. I would think myself that that is a rather narrow view of those particular circumstances, and I think one needs to look at a rather broader perspective. But there are two sides to that one; and I think that's an aspect of public confidence that one also needs to think about.

There's one final thing I'd like to say. I don't serve in or directly control either the Royal Ulster Constabulary or the British Army here; but in my experience (I only talk from a fairly detailed but limited time-span), we are talking about the use of lethal force in circumstances that are very carefully circumscribed (I'm glad to hear what Tom said about the yellow card). And the evidence I have seen (and you have to take my word for it, I suppose) is that it is only used in circumstances where life is at risk and the view of the people concerned is that there is no other way either to prevent the commission of an act or to deal with the circumstances. Of course, one could debate it, and it's quite proper we should debate the principle.

Ann McCann::
We've talked about Coagh and we've talked about terrorists being shot. I actually witnessed an incident myself, and I'm not sure whether the security forces felt they were IRA or whatever. We all have to presume these things, because we never really know what

really happens. But I presume the security forces thought the three men who were shot dead at the bookies at the Whiterock Road were IRA, and it turned out that they were petty criminals. I don't know how the army or (as everybody in West Belfast believes) the SAS who shot them could possibly have felt that their lives were in danger, when the man in the car didn't even have a gun.

John Ledlie:
Well, I don't think we want to debate the details of that, Ann.

Ann McCann:
But I have those details.

Robin Wilson:
Where's **your** evidence, John, for what you're saying? You're making an assertion that it is your firm belief that members of the security forces operate within the yellow card and only use such force as they have to in the circumstances, and never otherwise. Now there are plenty of us here who have plenty of contrary evidence, of which that case is one. The Yorkshire Television documentary interviewed eye-witnesses who gave a completely different account.

John Ledlie:
The evidence can only be based on what is actually in the police files, which contain, as far as they can gather, the full story; and which then go to the DPP – none of which material I see any more than you see. One can only go on what one is told about the incident in question; and indeed there may well be local people who have a closer knowledge because they may well have been there. If you were in the Whiterock Road area that day, Ann, you are probably better informed than I am. I quite understand that. But I can only go on the reports I see, the evidence I see, which is not the full legal evidence but the accounts that we have received.

Tom Hadden:
This is precisely the difficulty. None of us has the evidence. Why do we not have the evidence? Because we have a stupid inquest system. It doesn't produce the evidence that we should have in order to make these judgements. I wouldn't expect to find in the

police file a statement saying: 'We were proceeding along the road in a westerly direction, and we decided we would take out Mr X, and then we proceeded a little bit further and we took him out'. It doesn't happen that way.

Terry Shiels (The Law Society of Northern Ireland):
In those cases involving fatalities, which are ultimately the subject of criminal proceedings, directed against either the security forces or anybody else, the criminal proceeding precedes the inquest. I think that there are serious deficiencies in the inquest system; but I am also interested in whether there are serious deficiencies in the criminal system. In other words, presumably the court is the one medium, ideally, that can get at the truth of the matter. The question is: does it get at the truth?

Tom Hadden:
I mentioned earlier what I thought was a very serious deficiency in the criminal court system; and that is, it's murder or nothing. My position has always been that in many of these cases murder is not an appropriate charge, and the DPP is right not to say: 'I can get a conviction of murder'. In many of these cases, a jury or a judge is also right to say: 'It isn't really murder. It may have been man-slaughter, it may have been something else, but it's not murder'.

Sammy Douglas:
I think one thing that we need to agree on is that this policy of killing people certainly isn't sectarian or discriminating against one section of the community. As William has said this morning, several members of the Protestant community have been mur-dered by the security forces. I actually witnessed a car driving beside me and a fellow fell out of it who had just bombed a Catholic pub and he was shot dead by the army. I put myself in the position of those people who have the guns, the security forces; and if somebody goes to bomb a pub and they're driving away, I know my instinct would be to shoot them. Rightly or wrongly. I think that's another area we have to look at, in a personal sense. Forgetting about all these restrictions on the use of firearms, in a pragmatic way, in a life and death situation, if somebody's life is under threat, or somebody has murdered someone. I'm certainly not supporting a shoot-to-kill policy, but what I'm saying is that we need to think about the individual response in a situation like that also.

Kevin Boyle:

The best practice, the best response in a democratic society to this area of concern, is to do something about it, to inquire into the problem. As we have recently seen in Britain, arising out of a number of miscarriages of justice involving Irish people (though not exclusively Irish people), considerable inadequacies have emerged in the criminal justice system as a whole, which are now the subject of a Royal Commission; which I have no doubt will be probing and will come up with positive suggestions for changing what is basically a fundamentally good criminal justice system.

I feel that in the area of the use of firearms there is a need for a similar inquiry; not necessarily a Royal Commission, but a similar inquiry, both to deal with the question of the rules governing the use of certain types of firearms and to deal with the post-fatality situation – the inquest, for example – in the light of new international rules, which require a full public statement on what happened at a particular shooting, how it was investigated, and what's going to happen in the future. These are the new UN rules. There is a whole series of things, I think, that need to be looked at.

There's one point I personally think is an important one. I was involved in challenging these questionable shootings in Strasburg a number of years ago. When one looks at the source of the law that now exists, that is to say Section 3 of the Criminal Law Act, that law was adopted in 1967 as a general test to govern the use of force; and when that's an offence, you're charged with assault. But there was no discussion at all, in 1965, within the expert committee that drafted that legislation, of what might happen should a soldier or a police officer use firearms. It may seem to us now halcyon days, a long time ago. The Northern Ireland troubles hadn't begun. There were no such issues. This particular statute was drafted for Britain first, and was then applied to Northern Ireland. But I hope that one of the things that might happen is a specific enquiry not into the question of who killed whom in a particular case, but into the whole question of the way the legal system responds to what always begins with a question mark. Every death is unjustified until it's proved to be justified.

John Ledlie:

I do think that Tom Hadden made a very relevant and important point about inquests. It does seem to me that, in terms of public confidence, the very extensive delays that the present system imposes do make it very difficult, giving the impression of a cloak of secrecy around the whole thing, which is often not necessary, in my experience.

Tom Hadden:
Criminal proceedings come before the inquest, but only if somebody is quite quickly charged. If somebody isn't quite quickly charged, there's nothing to stop you having an inquest. And if, as a result of what appears at the inquest, you then change your mind, and you think that perhaps somebody should be charged, then you can go ahead and do it.

Terry Shiels:
I recall, in another incarnation in which I was particularly interested in these matters, that I was constantly exercised by the really extraordinary delay in the holding of inquests, even in cases in which no charges were directed. And I kept asking questions of the Authority as to why this was. Various explanations were vouchsafed, but the inevitable situation didn't change. Year succeeded year. And then, in the event, the legal machinery at the inquest was so deficient that really, in all practical terms, we could have done away with it, for all the relevance it contributed to the total situation. I think the whole question certainly needs addressed.

Francis Murphy (The Law Society of Northern Ireland):
There is no legal aid in Northern Ireland to help families who can't afford to employ lawyers to ask questions at inquests, when and if the inquest is finally held. What happens in Northern Ireland is that lawyers take on inquests for free, because of an interest that they have in other areas. One of the forms of discrimination that I'm very interested in is the question of access to proper legal advice and assistance. For instance, in Northern Ireland we have a situation where the right to silence has been very seriously restricted because of the Criminal Evidence Order. It was restricted here, but not in England and Wales.

And there are other issues where there may be discrimination against residents of Northern Ireland. In England and Wales, for instance, there are certain safeguards in relation to pre-trial advice and assistance, which are considered to be fundamental to the criminal justice system, but which don't operate at all in Northern

Ireland. For instance, we've recently had introduced in Northern
Ireland the Police and Criminal Evidence Order [PACE]. That
increases massively the powers of the police, and regulates the way
in which persons can be detained. It was introduced in England in
1986 and brought in in Northern Ireland in 1990. But in England
and Wales, it was felt that in order that the Police and Criminal
Evidence Act should properly function, and that the safeguards that
there are in PACE, which for the first time give people rights to legal
advice and assistance and access to a solicitor, should function
effectively, there should be a statutory duty solicitor scheme, whereby
the state would make a fund available for solicitors to be available
round-the-clock, so that any person who was arrested could get
directly in contact with a solicitor and be advised. And last year,
somewhere in the region of £25-27 million was spent to pay for the
statutory duty solicitor scheme in England and Wales.

The Police and Criminal Evidence Order was introduced in
Northern Ireland in a situation where, after the Criminal Evidence
Order had been brought in, the right to silence had been reduced,
and in a circumstance where you have many areas of disquiet about
the treatment of persons detained. We were told it was exactly the
same as the Police and Criminal Evidence Act in England and
Wales, but it was vastly different. For a start, it did not extend the
safeguards and rights of detained persons to those persons detained under the emergency provisions. They were completely
excluded. And secondly, there was no statutory duty solicitor
scheme. In fact, there were no provisions whatsoever for solicitors
to be available to advise persons held under the powers of PACE.
And I wonder why. Do we have a situation in Northern Ireland
where people don't need the same sorts of protection as in England
or Wales? In England and Wales, it was felt to be so important that
these provisions be there – so important to people's confidence in
the criminal justice system – that not only were they prepared to
spend nearly £30m to pay for solicitors, but they actually brought in
social scientists to study the operation of the access provisions.

I suggested that such a thing would be useful in Northern
Ireland and got a deadly silence. So here we are, eighteen months
after the introduction of PACE in Northern Ireland. There's no
independent research into how it's been operated. The police say
that 26,000 people were arrested and detained under PACE in the
first year of its operation in Northern Ireland, and we've no idea
what happened. Yet, in England and Wales, last year they spent

£27m in order to allow people to have access to legal advice and assistance. I find that very difficult to accept.

Kevin Boyle:
Well, regional discrimination certainly is a new discrimination category, but it does focus very interestingly on this area of the impact of the new laws on Police and Criminal Evidence, and the exclusion from PACE, as you say, of arrests under anti-terrorist laws. I'm glad that that's on the record. Could I ask now, leaving aside the Criminal Evidence Order, which in effect covers all trials, is there any sense in which there is a change in community perception of the Diplock Courts? Is the category 'sectarian' relevant to the discussion of the operation of the courts dealing with the terrorist emergency? It does seem to me that it's no longer an issue in those terms. Tom Hadden and I did some work in the early 70s, in which we did raise questions about differential sentencing, for example. But what do people feel? Is the perception in the community that the courts are unfair to Catholics as opposed to Protestants?

Bernard Cullen:
My sense is that that feeling lingers in some quarters, and that some politicians keep trying to flog that dead horse for their own purposes. But I don't hear many people raising it as an issue. Like Tom Hadden, I've never been absolutely committed to juries – especially in Northern Ireland. More specifically, I don't remember ever hearing a barrister or a solicitor involved in criminal cases in Northern Ireland who was prepared to say that they would rather have juries than Diplock courts. In order words, that they think they would get a fairer hearing for their client with a jury.

Kevin Boyle:
It's not that I distrust judges, but I'd be very much in favour of juries.

David McKittrick (British Irish Association; Ireland correspondent of *The Independent*):
I think what Bernard was saying is generally true. The contrast would be with, say, 1986, when the Irish Government was putting all that effort into trying to get three judges instead of one. That one didn't work, and there's no sign of it coming back. Partly

because the type of remarks by judges that Robin was talking about
have very largely died out. You don't get the 'posse' mentality
there so much any more. You've also had more Catholic judges
appointed in that time; and we've had the retirement of some of
the Protestant judges that exception was taken to. So while you've
still got the odd crusty type who wouldn't please all nationalists,
with the absence of supergrasses and suchlike now, the courts have
largely (though not entirely) been taken out of the political arena.

Noel Sinnamon:
I was speaking recently to a solicitor on our committee from the
South, and he put forward the view that as an Irishman he'd much
rather face a Diplock Court in Northern Ireland than go to a jury
trial in England.

Ann McCann:
We work with prisoners' families from both sections of the community, and we had a discussion one time with the wives (and a few
mothers) about the courts and how their husbands were sentenced. It was very interesting to see that hardly one of them even
realized that there was something different. They just accepted
that there would be a judge, and were quite surprised that in
England they would have a jury. But they came to the same
conclusion: they would prefer this unknown judge, rather than
people from the other community on a jury.

Kevin Boyle:
It would appear that the trial process now becomes a classic civil
liberties question, without any political or sectarian overlay. I would
certainly want to register my great concern on the Criminal Evidence Order, given the absence of juries; and the fact that the
Attorney-General has not accepted what I think is best practice, the
proper approach, which is that every case should start as a jury case,
unless he decides that it should be put before the Diplock Court.
This is a technical issue about what way you start the procedure. If
you work on the premise that emergency powers are exceptional,
then I would argue that the best operational way of doing that is to
'schedule in' rather than 'schedule out' cases for trial.
   Anyone want to raise any issues on prisons? Obviously, this is an
illustration of how the security controversies and problems
that arise vary over time. If this conference had been happening

at an earlier time, prisons would certainly have dominated our discussion.

Robin Wilson:
The reason why it's not dominating our discussion is precisely because of what's been done in the prisons. There are still some problems, but the system has been reformed.

Bill Webster:
An issue that we've been concerned about from the trade union angle is the question of the board of prison visitors. My trades council in Derry decided to nominate somebody as a prison visitor. This is going back to Gowrie's time. That man was turned down as a prison visitor. So there's also the question of who decides who'll be on the board of prison visitors.

Bernard Cullen:
I think that raises obliquely a question I hoped might emerge. That nominee was vetted. And the whole business of vetting of community groups illustrates again the point I've been trying to make all day: that the security and the political are all interwoven. You can't take one out of the context of the other. The same point applies to the political vetting, the behaviour of the troops and the police, lethal shootings, inquests, and so on. My worry is that there doesn't seem to be a realization at the highest level – at the highest political level and at the level of political advisers – that although they may have security successes today and tomorrow, the way in which the security successes are achieved stores up for them years of political backlash, political resentment and alienation, which in turn make their security job much more difficult.

They should always beware of anything that looks like a quick fix in security terms – and that includes vetting Glór na nGael and similar organizations, where there may well be a legitimate security worry. But if they achieve one security success in that area, they're likely to have thousands of people in the community who are potentially their allies become their enemies. To me, that's bad politics – and it's ultimately bad security policy.

Sammy Douglas:
The biggest group who were vetted were the Glencairn group, who lost about sixty workers under the ACE scheme. All the

authorities who withdrew their grant did was refer to Douglas Hurd's statement about the possibility of people being involved with paramilitaries, but those people had no opportunity to challenge the allegations that were made against them. And I think that's a real problem as regards the whole legal system: they don't know what they've done wrong. I know some groups who've actually gone back and said: 'Look, tell us who these people are who have links with paramilitary organizations, and we'll vote them off our committee. We'll vote new people on, if you want'.

Kevin Boyle:
This confirms again where I've got to in my own thinking: that more and more issues are about problems with the British constitution. The problems are basically structural. It's nothing to do with Northern Ireland, in other words, it's the problem of how you ensure accountability in the exercise of power. But before we finish, could I ask for a quick response on one final issue, the last point Tom Hadden raised? Should we recognize the paramilitaries to the extent that we would have a view of what was unacceptable paramilitary behaviour? This is a theme which is being discussed internationally, not in relation to Northern Ireland alone.

As you know, in many parts of the world there's a guerilla organization recognized to the extent that it has some standing – for example, the Palestine Liberation Organization, or earlier the ANC, or the force that has just taken over Ethiopia. The international rules would try to constrain not only the state but the opposing force, in terms of protecting civilians and ensuring that their behaviour does not breach the rules of war. Is this a runner in Northern Ireland at all, this idea that one should challenge the Provos and other paramilitaries in terms of the international rules of war?

Terry Shiels:
What sanctions do you impose?

Kevin Boyle:
There are no sanctions; but you simply address them, and say that this was defined as behaviour that was absolutely beyond the pale.

Noel Sinnamon:
I don't think that in a democracy - and I know there's a problem

about whether you can regard Northern Ireland as a true democracy – but in a democracy generally speaking, I don't think you can give people status because they shoot their way to the table. I think it would be a very dangerous precedent to do so in Northern Ireland. In other areas, where there's no possibility of democratic change, where reform by democratic means is blocked, you could say those people have a reasonable moral basis for their actions. But in a democracy, even an imperfect democracy, to allow people to shoot their way to a negotiating table is a very dangerous thing to allow to happen.

Terry O'Keeffe:
Kevin, in introducing this issue you asked: 'Should we recognize the paramilitaries?' I think that that's entirely the wrong way of putting it. If you think of why we should not use lethal force, there are very good pragmatic reasons for not shooting terrorists, for not having ambushes such as the one at Coagh; because it has political consequences which you won't like. There also may well be good legal reasons against using lethal force. But there seems to me to be also good moral reasons. There's a tremendous dearth of moral discussion now, twenty years on, about killing people. There's a certain moral outrage from one section of the community, for example, about three IRA men killed. Clerics will say: 'We'll have to look into this'. Whereas when an informer is shot, a few days later, there's actually no great moral outrage being expressed. At least, I haven't heard it. We've forgotten, I think, a whole level of moral outrage.

Now, how best do we bring that back? I don't think you bring it back by recognizing the IRA or the UDA as legitimate combatants in a civil war/insurgency. However, by publicizing codes of conduct, both for soldiers and civilians, you start the long process of reviving the moral discussion about how you should treat human beings and how you shouldn't treat human beings. I think the more that were to be introduced, by, for example, publishing and talking about the International Red Cross proposals, the better it would be. However, in a democracy, if you put it in terms of recognizing paramilitaries, giving them a status, people will lose the point.

Bill Webster:
I think it's entirely false to liken the behaviour of the paramilitary

organizations in this country to the likes of the ANC or the Tupamaros. I hear that every day in the areas where I work, and it's an absolute nonsense. But neither do I believe that the Provisional IRA or the loyalist paramilitaries are primarily responsible for what has taken place in this country; I don't accept that. I think they're a product of what has taken place over centuries, and I've tried to explain why they arise. But I fear that if we go along the path that's being proposed, we legitimize their actions. You legitimize the behaviour of individuals who go out and shoot working-class people, or shoot other people on the basis of their religion. I don't think we should have anything to do with that particular idea.

Kevin Boyle:
Well, we've had a quite penetrating discussion, from a broad range of positions. Thank you very much.

PART 3

REPORTS FROM THE WORKSHOPS
AND OPEN FORUM

DISCRIMINATION AGAINST WOMEN
Report to Conference

Tess Hurson

First of all, I have to confess that we have hoisted ourselves upon our own petard. We requested of Bernard that we go first, to unmarginalize ourselves, so to speak. The difficulty with that was that we talked right until four o'clock, so I have to apologize that the report that follows is something of a scramble. We did want to give as much time as we could to arriving at and working through recommendations that were sound and practical.

We had a very fruitful discussion in the morning. First of all, we asked the question – and it wasn't merely a rhetorical question – whether or not discrimination against women or inequality of opportunity did exist; and then, having arrived at the conclusion that it did, we tried to find out in what ways it existed, and why it existed. Participants then offered several concrete examples of discrimination and inequality – in the workplace, in the home, socially, in terms of the churches' response, and so on. We also tackled the question of why there was discrimination. And that led us, pretty logically, towards suggesting that there may be some longer-term solutions towards redressing inequality, mainly through the educative process. Concern with the more practical forms of inequality, alternatively, led us towards recommendations directed to redressing inequality in practical ways.

We thought that it might be better to tackle the educational side of things first, because the feeling of the group was that discriminations begin in school, and they then percolate all the way through adult life. We had a very good recommendation from John Watson. He proposed that teacher training be looked at a little bit more radically, and that people involved in this field should be starting to reorient the training ethos to take much more account of the inequalities that do exist, and of gender-based issues within that context. Female teachers, particularly, might be encouraged, during their training, to direct female pupils away from stereotyped female careers like: 'When I grow up, I'm going to be a wee nurse', or a wee teacher, towards a much more expansive notion of career possibilities. This recommendation was directed, not only to the Department of Education, but also specifically to principals, career teachers, and people involved in teacher training in Northern Ireland. As its first recommendation, then, the group called for a reorientation of teacher training and practice.

We also thought that, in the light of recent developments and potential developments – notably, that the Secretary of State is being encouraged to set up a commission on the status of women – another recommendation would be to the Secretary of State, calling upon him to put this commission into effect. We felt that this would be quite an important channelling group for the various research projects now being mooted which would focus on how gender was being handled currently in schools. It was further recommended that this commission for women act as a lobby to channel relevant research.

We then recommended that an inquiry be set up regarding the equality of opportunity for working-class children in Northern Ireland. This was on foot of the recent disclosures of discrimination against female children at the 11-plus stage. One member of our group drew attention to the fact – and I think that attention was drawn to this also in another group – that in working-class areas, there was a very tiny percentage (and specifically in the Greater Shankill area, thirteen children out of 373) who actually attained a pass in the 11-plus. So we recommended – to tie the recent disclosures together with other areas where a lot of other discriminations seemed to be occurring – that an inquiry be conducted, either by the Standing Advisory Commission on Human Rights, or by the Equal Opportunities Commission, or indeed by the proposed commission for women, to investigate the disproportionate failure rate of working-class female children in Northern Ireland.

We also looked at the whole area of adult education – a burgeoning area in Northern Ireland – and the vast population of that constituency by women. We would commend further education colleges and universities, and all those involved in the adult and higher education process, for the emphasis that is now being placed on tailoring courses to meet needs at community level, and particularly courses on self-development and access to third-level education. We would encourage them to develop a staged process, through which women could develop the foothold that they're gaining within this world; a foothold that may eventually lead to the workplace, if they wanted to go in that direction. We also recommended to FE colleges that they devote more resources to this area, and also involve the communities that they're living in, to make those communities much more aware of the input that they can have in developing and designing tailor-made courses for women, given that women make up one of their biggest groups of paying guests.

We also directed a recommendation to the churches and to the media, that there be a somewhat sharper monitoring of language – of nomenclature, if you like – when it is used about gender. There's still a fair amount of slippage on wee terms like 'chairs' and 'chairpersons' and 'chairmen' and 'chairwomen'. We didn't want to get into a massive semantic discussion. We simply wanted to register that while we acknowledge that the media and the churches have been making some strides in this direction, there's still a tendency to slip into a very sexist type of language, after a bit of tokenism.

We then went on to make some recommendations about the practical or short-term inequalities. We think that these are very important, because it's these sorts of indirect discriminations against women which end up disabling them at every level. We were also quite aware, in making these recommendations, that quite a few of them are applicable beyond the particular disablements and inequalities that affect women; that what we're saying may well have been registered in other workshops as well.

Dominica McGowan proposed that there be urgent movement on the provision of childcare facilities in Northern Ireland. In 1978, Lord Melchett, who was then the minister responsible, strongly recommended that nursery provision in Northern Ireland should be at least as good as it was elsewhere in the UK. Another investigation was conducted into all of this in 1988, which came up with more or less the same recommendations, and we understand that there is once again the atmosphere of inquiry. So, we wanted to take advantage of that, now that the subject is, so to speak, on the agenda, and to recommend to the minister, and indeed to the Secretary of State, that there be an urgent look at this whole question of childcare facilities. At present, there is no statutory childcare provision whatsoever in Northern Ireland. The very minimum recommendation is that childcare provision be created in Northern Ireland to the standard that is available across the water; and, beyond that, to follow another of the recommendations made by Lord Melchett, that an inter-agency consultative body be set up, which would include, for example, DHSS and DENI, as well as the various voluntary and community organizations involved, to determine precisely what childcare needs there are throughout Northern Ireland; and that this go hand in hand with a resource commitment to the setting up of adequate childcare facilities.

Now, the reason we made such a fuss about this was because it became very, very clear in the workshop that the lack of childcare facilities, while it may not seem a very big issue in itself, was a massively disabling factor for women returning to the workplace and for women trying to get into education which might develop them as people and also develop them financially, by giving them more independence; and that it was also very important because the lack of childcare facilities tended to reinforce role stereotypes, which saw women primarily as having the responsibility of caring for children, caring for elderly relatives, caring for disabled people. In short, the lack of childcare facilities reflected the prevalence of these sorts of outdated stereotypes of women, which women themselves did not necessarily subscribe to at all. So this was an important recommendation, not only at a practical level and in the shorter term, but also in the much longer term.

We had two final recommendations. John Fisher proposed a recommendation to the Secretary of State that a greater effort should be made to involve more women in the work of public bodies. And finally, we had a recommendation about carers. As I said, an awful lot of responsibility for looking after elderly relatives, disabled and the disadvantaged, falls on women. We felt that there should be far more resources allocated to community care – particularly given the recommendations of the Government White Paper and the emphasis on community care – and, more specifically, that there should also be bridging assistance for women, for example, in situations where the person who has been cared for dies: resources should be made available for counselling and retraining of women in these situations. Those recommendations would be made primarily to the DHSS.

POVERTY AND SOCIAL DISADVANTAGE
Report to Conference

Michael Brown

I must say that my brain doesn't work as clearly as the last speaker's; and therefore, you're not going to have anything like as full and detailed a report. Could I first of all pick out from Roisín's opening address, which we used as a base, three or four points which struck me. She made the point that a person's poverty was a person's exclusion from the minimum acceptable way of life in the member state in which they live. Then I picked out one or two other things, principally about community groups, who should have an effective say on an equal partnership basis: people in poverty are rarely consulted; they are suspicious of community activists and controllers of resources; and community participation should not be 'token'. She talked of many other things, but those were the things that I picked out straight away. Plus one other small point: that there was sufficient common ground on causes of poverty and conditions of poverty. People were pretty well in agreement with that.

Our group was a well-mixed group. We had the Reverend William Campbell from the Shankill Road Mission; we had NICVA; we had Work West; we had Mr Gusty Spence from the Shankill Activity Centre; Mr John McQuillan from the Greater Shankill Development Agency; we had a representative from the Northern Ireland Council for Travelling People, and a lot of others. We reckoned that acute poverty existed in Catholic communities rather than Protestant communities; but it was acknowledged that, of course, there was tremendous poverty in the Protestant communities also. I think the minister did actually say this recently, and we were in agreement with this. The 'who gets what' question is the most divisive one, because of the lack of available funds from Government. Very small amounts of money are available, and therefore there is tremendous competition for them. Competition for small amounts of money, lack of access to education, nothing to look forward to, the necessity of education for life within the community – those are some of the points made on that score.

But the point was also made that just chucking money about without community involvement is no good. Support from authority at all levels is essential, and money should be targeted to areas of the greatest deprivation. John McQuillan from Greater Shankill made the point that a fairer society, where resources are used where they're most needed, is what is required. He told us that he had been brought up in a very strong Protestant area of East Belfast, which is where I come from myself, and that he had been brought up in a society where Protestantism was 'it', and the Protestants were the people who ruled. He is now up the Shankill, saying that he has absolutely no problems at all about the allocation of resources where they are most needed, regardless of who gets them; and that is absolutely right. He also made the point that there are girls in the Shankill in such a state of poverty that they make a conscious decision to become pregnant, and thereby to rely solely on welfare benefits. According to Mr McQuillan, many of our sincerely held middle-class views just don't work in an area such as the Shankill, where over 70% are in receipt of one form of benefit or another. In Protestant areas, to ask for help is an admission of failure.

Let me pick out some of the other points that were made. Policy-makers have not so far been much influenced by the people who are worst affected. There was criticism of the established churches as having power and money in the community (I don't think our church does!); and people need to be given control of their own lives, rather than have them directed by such organizations. One participant claimed that the Government needs a population who are unemployed or uneducated so that they can direct our lives.

We talked a lot about the machinery for making representations to Government. This is always a very difficult one. The problem of who makes representations really suits Government, some people thought. The poor are not going to be able to achieve equality of opportunity, partly because of lack of funds, but there must be unified community campaigning, and it's no good relying on our politicians. The representative of NICVA told us that an anti-poverty network is being drawn together to campaign in conjunction with similar groups in GB. There is no trust, they tell us, in the people by Government, and therefore no trust by the people in Government. Government seems unwilling or unable to give the ordinary person on the street responsibility.

Our former President of the Irish Association, Professor McDonagh, felt that our problems are very similar here to those in the Republic. He quoted the case of the West, where there is no employment, and therefore no companionship; and so the community drifts and ceases almost to be a community. He also made the point that the basic divisions in Northern Ireland complicate the issue even more: if communities are polarized, they cannot release their full energies. The more people can work together, the more energy is released; and because of their coming together, more money becomes available from authority, in the nature of things. This energy must come from the bottom, from the people. Without a political commitment by Government to listen to anti-poverty groups, there will be no result from their efforts.

The Reverend Campbell, of the Shankill Road Mission, told us that if the community is disenfranchized by a system of direct government, there is no way really of changing political outlook. The Prime Minister isn't really too worried about what goes on in Northern Ireland. One member of our group stated that civil servants are running this Province rather than politicians. Many agreed that this was probably a fact. Some felt that it was very bad. Others felt that perhaps our politicians have been responsible for the mess that we're in, anyway.

Finally, Northern Ireland has a lot going for it, if we can really seriously institute a unified rethink on where we want to go, and organize the push, through forums such as today's, to reach an agreed target. Through pressure on elected representatives at every level, and by active community participation, then we may get somewhere. Unity is all important if we're to go ahead. Thank you.

DISCRIMINATION IN EMPLOYMENT
AND UNEMPLOYMENT
Report to Conference

Paul Bew

I think I should begin by being honest. The workshop on discrimination in employment and unemployment was probably (I intuit from the previous reports) a bit more divided than the two areas of poverty and gender that we've already heard about; and I think that was inevitable, given the nature of the discussion. I'm going to try and give a fair report of what was said at our group, but I think it's quite likely that some people may want to protest, so right away let me say, just protest!

I'm also going to begin by saying that there is one area in which we are agreed, and in which there is a recommendation from our workshop: that is, that what was variously called 'old-fashioned discrimination', 'direct' or 'brutal' discrimination – we didn't go in for euphemisms in our group – this phenomenon as it exists in Northern Ireland today is actually remarkably under-researched. It was accepted within the group that people actually do not know the extent of this phenomenon at this moment in time. I think that's the point at which we were all agreed. I suspect members of our group have intuitive views about how much the phenomenon continues to exist, and there would be disagreement on that point. But on the need for serious academic research to deal with that gap in the current literature and the current discussion, everybody was agreed.

There are a lot of difficulties in that type of research. Jamie Delargy (a current affairs producer for UTV) told us about how he had attempted to organize a television programme on this topic, and found that a lot of technical difficulties confronted him – for example, in getting the co-operation of schools, in creating CVs for testers in an application process. And there is no doubt that one of the reasons why research in this area has not been carried out so far is the number of technical difficulties that would face anybody trying to do it. But there did seem to be agreement that this is an area which requires further work; and it's really quite surprising, in view of all the other work that we know has gone on in the 'fair employment' area.

There is a second theme where there seemed to be a fair amount of agreement within the group: I think it's fair to say there was actually a tone of despair in what was said before lunch by Father Matt Wallace, and also by William Hutchinson from the Springvale project, about the employment situation in West Belfast. I think there was general agreement with Father Matt's phrase: 'We have reached saturation point with schemes'. And everybody sort of heaved at this point, and said: 'Oh, yes'. But that is perhaps not surprising.

There was also a marked pessimism. One of the points that came across was a feeling of wariness on the part of more than one commentator on the implications of Montupet; and particularly, about the number of jobs for unskilled and semi-skilled workers that would be created in the end. This is an area where there had been substantial hope, substantial optimism. Father Matt Wallace, Oliver Kearney, and others expressed doubts as to whether or not there would be the number of opportunities for unskilled workers that had originally been expected. At one point, Father Matt Wallace actually said, rather despairingly: 'Does anybody care?' In those two respects that I've outlined, there weren't fundamental divisions of attitude or approach.

But we did have major divisions. And I think that was really the value of the session, that it was stimulating and it wasn't repetitive or tedious; and the divisions really related to the whole question of fair employment strategy as it currently operates. Arthur Green, in particular (drawing on the work of Paul Compton [QUB] and on implications of some of the recent pieces by Graham Gudgin [Northern Ireland Economic Research Council]) argued that much of the imbalance in employment between the two communities in Northern Ireland could be related to structural factors. There are a whole number of points lurking around here. One is, of course, the whole role of the security industry, and what the employment profile of the two communities is if you take the security industry out.

One of the other points that were lurking around there was the whole question – almost mystically appearing and reappearing –

of the new Catholic middle class, which we never really got to grips with. Its actual size and extent we never really came to terms with. But I think everybody agreed it was potentially of very considerable political importance in Northern Ireland. From a different angle, William Hutchinson in particular stressed the Protestant working-class situation in West Belfast. And Linda Moore and others stressed the role of gender. One point that came across very forcefully indeed was that training for women in Northern Ireland really is appalling.

I have already said that Arthur challenged the whole basis of the fair employment strategy. He argued, in a broadly humanist sense, that there really is a problem about labelling people. He doubted whether this is what we should be trying to do at this time, and argued against its whole relevance. On the other hand, Oliver Kearney argued that the current policies are, in effect, simply not strong enough; that one of the distressing factors, as he saw it, is the fact that in the new and expanding areas of employment, Catholics are still not performing as well as hoped for.

Oliver argued that while in the late 1960s, in the late O'Neillite period, there was a broadly reformist attitude within the Protestant community, among Protestant employers, since 1974 there had actually been a hardening of attitudes, which was complicating this whole area. One of his most important points, at the end, was to say that, privately, senior civil servants had already acknowledged that within a few years the legislation that is currently on the statute-book would have to be 'beefed up' by strong affirmative action provisions.

That gives you some idea of the width of the argument within our group. And in the middle, reluctantly, but I have to say eloquently and resourcefully, Bob Cooper defended essentially the current policies. Now, a lot of our discussion was technical and quite detailed. I don't think it would be fair to inflict it on you at the end of a long day. Suffice it to say that the 1911 census raised its ugly head many times, and other crucial documents were discussed. I don't want to go into that. What I got a sense of from Bob, in a number of different interventions that he made, was a thesis which went something like this: that there is what he called an inner circle as regards employment, and the essential aim of fair employment strategy is to strip away the cumulative advantages, the privileges that relate to being inside that inner circle, and therefore to create equality of opportunity in that way.

When we talked about perceptions, and about the perception that the Fair Employment Commission is about creating jobs for Catholics, Bob did not deny this. He said this would not be a wildly inaccurate assumption on the part of sections of the Protestant masses. But he made the point that Protestants (particularly, the Protestant working-class community of West Belfast) who are outside the inner circle of cumulative advantage about jobs (recruitment by word of mouth, and so on) also stood to benefit from the erosion of the advantages that come from being within the inner circle of employment. That seemed to be the main theme that came across in his defence of the current strategy of the Government.

So, I think I've said enough to show that there was a lot of debate. It was a fairly lively and intriguing group. I would like to say, on behalf of the Irish Association, that I'm very grateful to all the people who came and gave us the benefit of their ideas, because it certainly wasn't an insipid discussion, as these discussions sometimes are. Some of the issues we did not solve. In fact, hardly any of them did we solve. But I hope you can see that it was a good and useful discussion.

EMERGENCY LEGISLATION AND THE
ADMINISTRATION OF JUSTICE
Report to Conference

Robin Wilson

Our group, like Paul's, was sharply divided. Basically, the division was: on the one side, most people in the group; on the other, our poor friends from the Northern Ireland Office. I know that wouldn't have happened twenty years ago, and it really was a very salutary demonstration of the significance of the fact that since 1972 we've had direct rule. During that time, issues of security have been entirely controlled by the British authorities, a time during which at least some sections of the Protestant community – as there was some very eloquent testimony today – have suffered some rather unpleasant experiences at the hands of the security forces themselves. The upshot of all that was a rather broadly civil libertarian consensus throughout the group – at least amongst those who talked – extending to a restrained anger, in the form which Tom was expressing this morning; and of which John Ledlie was unfortunately in the position of being, through no fault of his own, the butt.

There were seven issues which we addressed. One was a question which Tom mentioned this morning: is it unrealistic (as Tom suggested it is) to think of a situation where you didn't need emergency legislation in Northern Ireland? And, surprisingly, there was actually quite a strongly held view in our group that one couldn't compromise on principles of justice: the situation couldn't be allowed to arise where one accepted that an emergency became normal, where one accepted emergency legislation for an indefinite period. And at the very least, as Kevin Boyle expressed it, there was a feeling that one surely has to make every effort to minimize departures from the rule of law as conventionally understood.

The second question that came up was again one that Tom had raised this morning: is there 'a security solution'? Bernard Cullen pointed out that actually this tends not to be the view of most actually existing people in the security forces. It tends to be only some politicians who believe there is a security solution. And he said that their facile demands over several years for the security forces to go into certain areas and 'take out the terrorists' have only served to make things worse. He also suggested, however, that, even if there was a political settlement, that in itself would not eliminate entirely the security problem. That is to say, if there is no 'security solution', there is no solely political solution either, because, as he put it, there will always be a handful of people around who would still want to turn to the use of guns. But that shouldn't panic us into having a whole panoply of authoritarian legislation indefinitely to deal with it.

This discussion about politics and security then led on inevitably, in the current context in which we meet, to a discussion of the prevailing political vacuum. I think there was a reasonable consensus on this: people felt that the continuance of a political vacuum was a reflection of the degree to which the conventional politicians in Northern Ireland themselves must bear a major responsibility for the perpetuation of the security problem.

The third question we looked at was harassment, which in fact we probably spent longer on than anything else. It was Bernard who said that, even more than the misuse or the alleged misuse of lethal force by the security forces at various times, the humdrum, day-to-day, stupid, gratuitous harassment that people (especially young people) experience is probably the biggest single recruiting sergeant for the paramilitary groups. This led on to a discussion of whether or not the army can be adequately trained to operate in a more courteous way to members of the civilian population; or indeed, whether the army is appropriate for this kind of activity at all.

But people also felt that, even if the army was to be withdrawn from the situation (and there was a view that the army should be withdrawn from the streets), police culture in Northern Ireland has been so influenced by the troubles that there are a whole set of problems there too, in terms of relations between the police and members of the public. There was some black humour about the fact that the only redeeming feature seems to be that this is rather more cross-sectarian than in the past. In other words, it isn't so much that the police are better than in the past, but that they just don't discriminate any more!

There was, however, a point made, again by Bernard (as it happens), that it should be recognized that amidst all these complaints about the behaviour of the police, there is, in fact, quite a wide range of attitudes to the police within communities in Northern Ireland, including communities in West Belfast; and that, indeed, often people's complaint about the police in West Belfast isn't that they are harassing them, but that they aren't doing their job.

This led on to a discussion about the Independent Commission for Police Complaints, whose representative told us about the outreach work they're doing, to schools, to community groups, and so on, to explain their work. But the response of Ann McCann, from the Peace People, was to say: 'Where's the beef?' She wanted to see more evidence that action was being taken against recalcitrant officers before she would be persuaded. There was also a discussion about the issue of whether the police could ever be acceptable if the controlling bodies are not representative. And so the issue was raised whether the SDLP should continue to maintain its boycott of the Police Authority.

The fourth area we looked at, and one which provoked a lot of discussion, was the use of lethal force, which again touched on the question of the appropriateness or otherwise of the army in dealing with the situation in Northern Ireland, because of their training to use maximum rather than minimum force. Tom Hadden suggested, in the context of arguments about whether there might or might not be a 'shoot-to-kill' policy, that there might be certain incidents that had taken place in which there had been a view taken at meetings, at whatever level (one never knew), that it might be no harm if the incident was to end with fatalities rather than arrests. He also expressed concern that there were certain incidents – and I imagine he was thinking, for example, of the recent killings in Coagh, though he also mentioned the shootings in 1982 by the RUC in County Armagh – where there was a suggestion that there was an element of revenge or hitting back for previous paramilitary attacks on the security forces.

There was a long discussion about the problems of various aspects of the use of lethal force – for example, the fact that one never knows whether soldiers do or do not operate according to the instructions of the yellow card that they carry. We also

discussed the inadequacy, as Tom said this morning, of the 1967
Criminal Law Act, which only requires the force used by police or
soldiers to be 'reasonable in the circumstances', rather than 'minimum force'. There was also the fact that the Director of Public
Prosecutions is very reluctant to support the idea of prosecutions
of members of the security forces, which Tom feels he or she
might be more likely to do were there to be a provision for the
possibility of a manslaughter charge as well as a murder charge.

At this point, John Ledlie felt that the NIO might make some
response. He did accept that there are issues of public confidence
at stake here. He was prepared to countenance the idea that
perhaps the criteria which the DPP uses in deciding whether to
prosecute or not could be looked at. And he also suggested that
the adequacy of inquests in Northern Ireland might be something
that could be reviewed in some way.

The upshot of this discussion was a proposal, which I think came
from Kevin Boyle, that the whole question of the use of force by
the police and the army, and the operation of inquests and so on,
could legitimately be the subject of some kind of fundamental
inquiry – perhaps under a senior judge. There are clearly a whole
number of issues here, not in terms of this or that particular
shooting, but a whole number of issues which have to be teased
out with some degree of seriousness; and perhaps this might be
conveyed back to the powers-that-be by our friends that are here
from the NIO today.

A fifth issue, that was only briefly touched on, was, irrespective
of the use of lethal force by the police and army, what one does
about lethal force by members of paramilitary groups. The argument was expressed that perhaps we ought to have some kind of
code of conduct for them too. There was a division of opinion on
this. Some people felt that this would actually expose the IRA or
the UVF or whoever to a serious moral challenge as to their
activities. On the other hand, there was the view that this would
merely legitimize their operation.

Two other items were the courts and the prisons. In terms of
both of these, there was a feeling that what had previously been
very substantial grievances had largely been defused over the
years. For example, in terms of the courts, there were more Catholic judges than in the past, we didn't have the supergrass system
any more, and so on. There was, however, a division of opinion
between those who wanted to see a restoration of jury trial as an

objective, or at least to see the practice instituted that cases should be 'certified in' rather than 'certified out' – that is to say, that the presumption should be in favour of a jury trial rather than in favour of non-jury Diplock courts – and the majority opinion that the current system is OK. I say the majority opinion: it wasn't mine, and it wasn't Kevin's; but I think it was the majority view.

On prisons, there was the feeling that most of the issues had been defused. Then a discussion about an individual case of someone who had been blocked from membership of the board of prison visitors by the security authorities led into a more general concluding discussion about politics and security in Northern Ireland, and the whole apparatus of vetting and secrecy which prevails, the lack of accountability, and so on.

There was one final point, which I think is worth quoting Bernard yet again on. It was a kind of passionate statement at the end, which I think quite a few of us in the group shared: it is apparently still not realized, at the highest level in Government, that while it may be possible to have a security success today or tomorrow, it may well be at the cost of thousands of potential friends and supporters lost and years and years of backlash stored up for the future.

OPEN FORUM

Bernard Cullen:
Perhaps I should point out that there were other people in our
workshop! I must say, I didn't expect to be quoted quite as much.
In any case, our thanks go to all four rapporteurs for their admira-
bly crystalline and stimulating reports.

Now, the floor is completely open, both to those who have
recently joined us and to others who were in workshops earlier
in the day. You may feel that one of your own subtle points was lost
in the synopsis; or you may want to take the discussion a bit
further.

Francis Murphy:
For the last ten years, I've worked in Belfast Magistrates Court,
which is the busiest magistrates court in Northern Ireland, with
58% of all adult criminal prosecutions and 59% of all juveniles.
And over that time, I've been very conscious that that system
discriminates against poor people; against poor males, especially.
And one discriminatory factor that hasn't changed, through all of
the well-meaning discussions and work that has been done in
looking at structures in Northern Ireland, is that, in terms of
access to good advice, the poor in Northern Ireland are still
discriminated against – no matter whether they live on the Shankill
Road or in Andersonstown.

There are those who say that to look for help is to admit failure.
But good advisors can create supportive relationships, which help
people to grow rather than become dependent. It's quite clear, in
Northern Ireland, that the legal talents that we have are on a par
with, if not better than, anywhere else in Western Europe; yet the
structure of our advice services is such that if you are poor, the
access that you have to effective advice, on issues which directly
relate to you, is very limited. You can go, if you've the money, to a

good solicitor, you can get a great barrister to talk to you about your financial affairs. But if you're on the Shankill Road or elsewhere in West Belfast and you've got complicated problems in relation to your family and your benefits, in terms of mental health, or anything like that, you have a very limited access to advice.

In England and Wales, there has been a major debate over the last six years on the future of legal aid, which finances the majority of legal services which poor people have access to. Over those six years, there has been major research on the effectiveness of legal aid systems. But none of that research extended to Northern Ireland. Yet the same decisions which affect people in Britain are going to come in in Northern Ireland, without any research.

Recently, the Belfast Citizens Advice Bureaux, which handle major problems, had to close two bureaux in Belfast: one in the Whiterock, in the middle of Ballymurphy; and the other in Botanic Avenue, which dealt with Lower Ormeau and the problems of people who rent flats. They had to close those bureaux because of a lack of funding. The Belfast Unemployed Centre has to deal with major problems of people who are made redundant, but they are underfunded too. The whole question of advice service funding is a major discrimination, because the problems that poor people have are never given due consideration.

Belfast Magistrates Court is a perfect example of this discrimination between rich and poor. Across the street from Belfast Magistrates Court are the Royal Courts of Justice, the High Court. It's a beautiful place. It has a restaurant. There's space. You can sit and talk. Go into Belfast Magistrates Court, which is reckoned to be the busiest court in Western Europe, and you can't even get a cup of tea. There's nowhere you can sit quietly and talk. There are no facilities for women with children. The toilets are filthy. You're packed together – witnesses, defendants, accused, all together in one place.

It's apparent to anybody who works in the advice field that a small amount of consistently directed funding to that area does an awful lot for the large numbers of people who come through the doors of the advice agencies, which are constantly under pressure about whether or not they can open tomorrow. Without a proper advice service, without adequate access to adequate advice, you disenfranchize whole sections of people and leave them feeling powerless and frustrated.

Michael Brown:
Could I just add to that? Recently, I was involved in those courts
with a young fellow from Derry who was up on a charge. I had
exactly this experience. He was using legal aid. We suddenly
discovered that the solicitor he had originally been allocated had
handed over to another one without telling anybody. We found
the other one in court. He was advising this fellow to plead guilty
when he should never have done. It wasn't until I went down
myself and spoke very sternly indeed to this solicitor that he began
to take notice; and in fact, did a very good job in the end. But he
was going to try and get away with murder.

Jim McCorry (Extern Organization):
I have two questions for Robin. The first one is: given the introduction of the Police and Criminal Evidence Order here, did your
workshop discuss the whole relationship between the need for
emergency powers and the quite extensive powers that are allowed
to the police under that order? The second thing is that there
seems to have been a couple of benefits from that order since it
was introduced. One is that the conditions inside the police station have certainly been improved, and we're getting much easier
access, particularly to young people. But this seems to have unintended consequences, in that instead of beating up young people
inside police stations, they're getting beaten up now before they
get there. I'd like to know if they discussed that in the workshop.
And did they look at the possibility of finding out how many
complaints are made against the RUC and then withdrawn?

Robin Wilson:
That order was mentioned, but only very briefly. It was noted that
it doesn't yet apply to the interrogation of terrorist suspects; and
also that the right to silence was no longer guaranteed.

Bernard Cullen:
There was also the question about complaints that have been
made and are withdrawn before they're processed. I'm sure those
statistics are available somewhere.

Francis Murphy:
Unfortunately not, Bernard. The point is that when PACE was
brought in, unlike England and Wales, there was no structured

research introduced alongside it to monitor how PACE actually operates. We're eighteen months into the operation of PACE, and there is no research. There might well be statistics, but they belong to the RUC; and there is no statutory obligation on them to publish those statistics, or any statistics, or to say what sort of statistics they should gather.

Bob Cormack:
Just a brief comment, perhaps to give Francis some good news. I'm speaking now as chair of Belfast Citizens Advice Bureaux. As a result of closing down those two bureaux, we managed to exert sufficient pressure on the Department of Education that they produced £200,000, and we have just opened a new bureau in West Belfast.

Tess Hurson:
One recommendation was made by our group, and I didn't have time to register it. That was, that the Irish Association themselves look at the issue of the presidency of the Association. If they take a wee look down their list, they'll see that there has been only one woman president.

Michael Brown:
The point was made, in one of the reports, about problems of employment at Montupet. I have a son working for a subsidiary, and I asked him only the other day about the figures for employment at Montupet. He said it's about 200 at the moment. The problem about getting that figure up is the slowness in getting people trained. They have to go to France.

Robin Wilson:
The problem that arose at Montupet was that advertisements appeared in the press for general machinist jobs; but they were demanding a year's experience in a similar engineering environment, which obviously most people in West Belfast don't have.

Martin O'Brien (News and Current Affairs Producer, BBC NI):
I would like to pick up one point; and I wonder if someone is still here from the Independent Commission for Police Complaints. I was interested to hear about the Commission's outreach to schools, and I'd like to hear a bit more about it. The Commission come

across to me as people who are trying very hard to be seen to be independent, and trying very hard to win the confidence of the community. But I just wonder how aware are they of the impression that many of us have that they are lacking the teeth necessary to do their job properly and to tackle the type of petty harassment that has been referred to earlier.

Bernard Cullen:
I can report that the representative of the Commission had to leave about two minutes ago.

John Ledlie (Northern Ireland Office):
I don't represent the Commission, but I can certainly arrange for that dialogue to take place. I see them from time to time. I think that the point that has just been made is an important one. It's a question of looking at the way that body does its work within its terms of reference. It is a comparatively new body, but they have within the past year or so produced a couple of reports; and there's quite a lot that I'm sure they would be delighted to talk to you about, about the way they do their job.

I think they feel quite strongly, as it came out in our group, that within their terms of reference they do all they can. There is a question of public perceptions and public profile, which is an interesting one to debate. And then there's the second question you raised, about whether their terms of reference are as wide as all the community would want. Then you get into the quite difficult territory of the relationship between the Commission and the police themselves, and whether it's their job to get into questions of police discipline; or whether, as is the current situation, they look only at complaints made against the police. And that takes us into the territory of complaints that have been withdrawn. It's a very interesting and important area, and we can certainly discuss that. I'm afraid I'm not the right person to answer all your questions this afternoon. But we can certainly arrange it.

Martin O'Brien:
Thank you very much. I'll follow that up.

Jean Murray:
Just to pick up on the question of the withdrawn complaints. I wonder if the speaker was actually thinking of a number of

complaints that are now being informally resolved. In the matter of complaints against the police, the Police Authority has only an oversight function, in terms of looking at statistics and trends and things like that. But one of the things the Authority has been trying to encourage is a greater use of informal resolution. I just wondered if that was what this gentleman here was talking about.

Jim McCorry:
I'm talking about incidents where young people make complaints and are then accused by the police of assaulting the police. The case against the young person is brought to court by the police before the complaint is even heard, and the young person is bribed or blackmailed into actually withdrawing the complaint. I'm not talking about an isolated incident. This has happened on a regular basis. That is not informal resolution.

Jean Murray:
I would be very concerned about cases like that. I have heard of similar cases to this one; but the point is that the complainant does actually sign a statement. Now, I know that you're suggesting that there's a certain amount of duress for people to sign that statement. But within its brief of overseeing complaints, the Authority sees a file in front of it that has a signed statement from someone saying that they are withdrawing their complaint. So it's very hard in that situation to know whether or not this is a genuine withdrawal. There are lots of genuine cases of people having changed their minds, for whatever reason. So, while I recognize and would be concerned about the issue that you raise, on the basis of the sort of anecdotal evidence you're talking about, it's very difficult to know how to get to grips with that situation.

Jim McCorry:
If we were getting the figures from the Commission, and actually allowing young people to respond without being harassed afterwards – and I'm sure we could arrange for some sort of protection to enable them to do that – the evidence would not be anecdotal. I've had young people literally crying in court, because I had to convince them to plead guilty, knowing that they were going to get six months; and a barrister saying: 'Look, I'm not here to get you justice, I'm here to get the best deal that we can'. And this isn't one incident. There's now a pattern of young people being beaten up

prior to going into custody, and then being forced to withdraw complaints; and it is worrying. In terms of the police image, it's having an effect on that community.

Francis Murphy:
This was one of the issues that the statutory duty solicitor scheme in England and Wales was designed to avoid; and the research that was set in train was to look at issues like that. But PACE has been brought in in Northern Ireland, and no formal arrangement has been made for the protection of juveniles. Because there was no statutory duty solicitor scheme, and no relevant adult organization, this issue has been building up in the past eighteen months, because of the powers that are granted under PACE which are not monitored.

CHAIRMAN'S CLOSING REMARKS

Bernard Cullen

Thank you all for your contributions. These points certainly do underline the importance of the issue that Martin O'Brien raised: namely, how imperative it is that bodies such as the Police Authority and the Independent Commission for Police Complaints actually have teeth. Related to that is the crucially important question of public perception. As Ann McCann said in our workshop, when a member of the Independent Commission referred to the reports they have published: 'But nobody where I live reads any of these reports'. Those bodies will have to devise some alternative means of communicating effectively to disaffected citizens how they have been carrying out their statutory duties, even within their restricted terms of reference.

It has been a long day, and I think we are all tired. Of course, most people I spoke to during the tea break remarked that we just didn't have enough time to do justice to all the issues that have been raised today; and one of the workshops went on until after four.

Paul said earlier that we didn't solve all the problems. I'd have been absolutely astounded if we had solved **any** problems in a day. If we have helped to bring some of those problems out into the open, and onto the table for discussion, I believe we have achieved a good deal. It is my own conviction that a society that harbours in its midst a number of substantial groups which nurse their grievances, keep them to themselves, keep them festering in the ghetto (including the ghetto of the mind), and doesn't bring those grievances out for public discussion, is not a healthy society; and to the extent that we in Northern Ireland in recent years have failed to do that, that's an instructive measure of the pathology of our society. In this respect, we are a sick society. We must face up, fearlessly and candidly, to the grievances carried by the marginalized in our community – though that involves making oneself vulnerable, and even exposing oneself to the accusation of being a propagandist for the terrorists. If the Irish Association can play any part in carrying on the process of bringing these divisive and often hurtful issues out into the open for discussion, we are very pleased to be of service and to offer a forum and a platform.

What I think we have achieved, in the face of some sincerely held reservations about holding a conference like this at all, is that we have demonstrated that we can – in spite of the widespread and deeply ingrained divisions in Northern Ireland – bring together a diverse group of people, with very deeply held views, and we can discuss a range of matters which have divided us in this part of Ireland for at least two generations. We can not only talk to each other, but perhaps even more important, we can listen to each other. We have demonstrated that we can talk about matters of life and death as well as bread and butter, child care, employment, livelihood, poverty, and so on, without coming to blows; and without pulling any punches. Certainly, there were no punches pulled in the group I was in, and from the reports we've all heard there were no punches pulled in the other groups either.

But no matter how good and worthwhile today's conference has been, to bring you together for a day's discussion and simply leave it at that would be deeply unsatisfactory, because so many of the issues raised have been left up in the air. I would like to see the process begun today carried on and developed. With that in mind, the Irish Association is planning to make this the first of a series of similar meetings, devoted to similarly contentious issues. We don't have to attempt to repeat this kind of all-embracing, many-pronged conference; we shall probably arrange conferences or smaller workshop-type meetings focused more precisely on particular issues.

And there's another element in our planning. Having laid before some of our senior public servants our dissatisfactions with various aspects of the way in which we are governed, I think it entirely reasonable to give them an opportunity, at some time in the future, to come back to us, and report to us what they have done in the meantime to take account of the points that were made to them in the course of today's conference.

The Irish Association is committed to dialogue: dialogue particularly between and among people who do not instinctively agree with each other on political matters. And if we can do anything to help foster that dialogue, we are here to serve the community in Ireland, north and south.

Just before I wrap things up, there are a number of people it is my pleasant duty to thank. This is where this begins to sound like my Oscar acceptance speech. On your behalf, I want to thank again our speakers this morning – Roisín McDonough and Tom Hadden. Really, without their invigorating start to the day we wouldn't have achieved as much progress as we did. I also want to thank the chairpersons – the chairmen and chairwoman – of our workshops, and the workshop rapporteurs. Like our keynote speakers, they were also dragooned into service at very short notice, and I'm very grateful to them.

I'd especially like to thank the director of the Irish Association, Barbara FitzGerald, for her enormous support to me in planning the conference; and equally helpful was the executive secretary of the British Irish Association, Marigold Johnson. There are also people here who were of invaluable assistance in helping me to compile the list of people to be invited today. I won't embarrass them by naming them – you know who you are, and I'm very grateful to you. I want to thank the Gulbenkian Foundation, without whom it really would not have been possible, since they financed today's conference. Most of all, I want to thank you for agreeing to give up your Saturday. Without you, of course, the whole event would not have happened; and I hope you have found your sacrifice worthwhile. Finally, I wish you all a safe journey home, and I hope to see you all at the next Irish Association conference. Slán abhaile.

BIOGRAPHICAL NOTES

Paul Bew
President of the Irish Association and professor of politics at The
Queen's University of Belfast. Author of a number of books,
including *Conflict and Conciliation in Ireland.*

Kevin Boyle
Professor of law and Director of the Human Rights Centre at The
University of Essex. Co-author (with Tom Hadden) of *The Anglo-
Irish Agreement: A Commentary.* A member of the executive commit-
tee of the British Irish Association.

Michael Brown, OBE
A member of Belfast City Council from 1973 until his retirement
in 1985.

Bob Cormack
Head of the Department of Sociology and Social Policy at The
Queen's University of Belfast and co-editor (with R. D. Osborne)
of *Public Policy and Discrimination in Northern Ireland.*

Bernard Cullen
A Vice-President and President-Elect of the Irish Association, President of the Irish Philosophical Society, and professor of philoso-
phy at The Queen's University of Belfast.

Brian Garrett
A solicitor practising in Belfast and a past President of the Irish
Association (1986–1988). Former Chairman of the Northern Ire-
land Labour Party. Former member of the Standing Advisory
Commission on Human Rights.

Tom Hadden
Professor of law at The Queen's University of Belfast and co-author (with Kevin Boyle) of *Ireland: A Positive Proposal.* A member of the Standing Advisory Commission on Human Rights from 1986 to 1991.

Tess Hurson
Information Officer with the Rural Development Council for Northern Ireland. Formerly conference organizer/administrator with the Fortnight Educational Trust.

Roisín McDonough
Project Director of the Brownlow Community Trust, Craigavon.

Robin Wilson
Editor of *Fortnight* and Secretary of Initiative '92.